"Through this beautiful collection of learning stories, Deb Curtis paves the way for us to begin to explore some of the questions central to our work as educators. What will inspire teachers and families to find joy in observing children? What will help adults see how vital our understanding of children is to our own development as a species? What might support changes in the way we design curriculum and environments for our youngest learners? The answers to these questions have to be layered with the complexity that only an exceptional professional, insightful observer, and remarkable storyteller can offer.

These stories and photographs illustrate children's brilliancy. Through thoughtful analysis, Deb helps deepen our understanding about children's learning and our role as facilitators of this learning. She also inspires us to discover how we too, can learn alongside children. I can't wait to start using this book with all of the teachers and families I serve. Once again, Deb has managed to engage my heart and my intellect in a way that makes me want to be better at what I do."

~Eliana Elias, *M.A., Early Childhood Coach and Instructor*

"I will always hold dear in my heart the first 'Really Seeing Children' article I read in 2008. I wished that I could see children in the way that Deb Curtis described. Working closely with Deb, and reading the wonderful collection of stories she shares in this book, have helped transform my teaching practice. Learning to take the time to pause and marvel, I now see children's competencies and their big ideas come alive."

~Nadia Jaboneta, *Preschool Teacher*

These articles were originally published in *Exchange* magazine.
Exchange is a bimonthly management magazine for directors, owners, and
teachers of early childhood programs. For more information about *Exchange*
and other Exchange Press publications for directors and teachers, contact:

Exchange Press
7700 A Street
Lincoln, NE 68510
(800) 221-2864 • www.ChildCareExchange.com

ISBN 978-0-942702-64-4

Printed in Korea by Four Colour Print Group, Louisville, Kentucky

© Dimensions Educational Research Foundation, 2017

Cover and interior design by Kaitlyn Nelsen and Stacy Hadley,
    Dimensions Educational Research Foundation
Cover photo by Matthew Lawrence
Typeset in the Bell Gothic and Bembo typefaces
Interior photos by Andrea Parypa, Deb Curtis, Kate Tucker,
    Matthew Lawrence, and Nadia Jaboneta

Really Seeing Children

Really Seeing Children

A collection of teaching and learning stories to inspire an everyday practice of reflection, observation, and joyful presence with children

Deb Curtis

Dear Salmonberries,
(Louisa Carmichael, Paige Choi, Sydney Choi, Sawyer Hua, Emily Johnson, Opal Joisher, Garvey Livingston, Yveline Mauger, Tole Newell, Julian Rhodes, Ryan Rivera, and Jonah Sell)

I'm dedicating this book to you. Of my many, many years as a teacher, these last two years with you have been among the most joyful and meaningful of my career. From the time you were toddlers, there has been something special about the way you have lived and learned together. You have taught me how to delight in simple wonders, laugh often, engage fully with my senses, dive in fiercely to focus and learn, and most of all, how to cultivate deep relationships through both loving and spicy moments. I truly believe that what you know about getting along with others is the key to democracy and world peace. Thank you for all you have given me and each other. I will continue to spread your wisdom through sharing stories of your amazing ways together.

Love,

Jes

Acknowledgments

I'd like to thank my colleagues Jess Guiney, Lorrie Baird, Sheena Wilton, Kate Tucker, Nadia Jaboneta, Andrea Parypa, and the Bright Beginnings Toddler Cohort for thinking and writing with me about our deep appreciation of the children in our lives.

Special thanks to Bonnie Neugebauer, who invited me to contribute to *Exchange* magazine for many years. My "Really Seeing Children" articles are my favorite of all I have written. Carole White and Donna Rafanello were terrific editors and supporters of the original articles. I'm grateful to Emily Rose, who has been a champion to make the vision I have for helping others really see children into this beautiful book. Special thank you to Stacy Hadley and Kaitlyn Nelsen, who shared their creativity and skills to help all of us really see children through their amazing design work for the book.

To the families of the Salmonberry children: You have shared your hopes and dreams, as well as your worries and struggles, and have always been open and supportive of my work with your children. What great kids you have brought into the world!

I am grateful for my co-teachers, Belinda Berg, Kate Tucker, Melody Dayton, Rebecca Adrian, and Megan Arnim, who have shared this dreamy group of children with me over the past two years. Particular appreciation goes to Matthew Lawrence, who took several of the photos in the book, including the cover, and is always eager to play, think, and marvel with me in our work together.

And as always, to my family, Lonnie and Casey, who are good sports about listening to my stories about children, and to Margie Carter, who continually challenges and enriches my life. I'm forever grateful.

Contents

Section 2

Planning Environments to Help You See Children

Section 3

Seeing Children with Others

Section 4

Seeing Children and Theories
of Development

Section 5

Sharing the Stories
of Seeing Children

INTRODUCTION
An Invitation to Really See Children

I wonder what 22-month-old Emily has on her mind as she maneuvers and uses her whole body to lift the wooden stool. It's nearly as big as she is and probably weighs almost as much. With her muscles flexed and a determined look on her face, she uses great effort to carry the stool across the room to the small table in our drama area. She pushes it in close and then works at the difficult challenge of getting herself up onto the stool to begin her tea party.

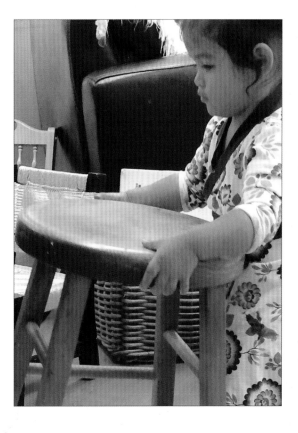

I regularly see Emily work to lift heavy objects and take on other physical and intellectual challenges in our room. Capturing the details of these moments over time adds to my growing appreciation and knowledge of her initiative, fortitude, and cognitive and physical skills. When Emily repeatedly asks to read the book *Mothers Can Do Anything*, I marvel at the vision she has for herself at such a young age.[1] Taking time to see Emily's amazing ways prompts me to notice and enhance the meaning the book may have for her. We share in the excitement of seeing possibilities for Emily in the powerful female pilots, engineers, and fire-fighters pictured in the book.

This ordinary, yet significant story of Emily is one of many I have been fortunate to collect about children over my long career as an early childhood educator. Children bring pleasure, never-ending curiosity, and are always present and fully engaged. Sharing in their world has expanded my life and continually engages me intellectually, emotionally, and spiritually. Taking time to cultivate the ability to really see children has enhanced my work in so many ways. I am grateful for the opportunity to share these stories of children and I hope they will inspire you to collect your own stories—the benefits are practical as well as deeply nourishing:

- Seeing children is about seeing the details of their remarkable ideas and actions. Studying what you observe and seeing yourself as a teacher-researcher to find children's skills and competencies enhances your own professional development and informs your practice when responding and planning for children. Seeing children's astonishing ways brings the joy and wonder back to your teaching.

- When you share the details of what you see with children they feel known and their confidence and competence grows. Helping children to see themselves promotes self-regulation and initiative, as well as helps them see themselves in relationship to others.

- Sharing the stories of children's ideas and actions with families and other educators invites them to pause and marvel with you about children's competence and helps them see the important learning that happens in your program.

Slow Down and Study

Nobody sees a flower—really—it is so small it takes time—we haven't time—and to see takes time, like to have a friend takes time.

~Georgia O'Keeffe

As Georgia O'Keeffe says, "to see takes time" and this is true for seeing children. It takes time, discipline, and ongoing practice to slow down and see the details of what is unfolding in your busy days with children. You must do the difficult task of suspending your own agenda from moment to moment to really see children's points of view and actions. To help you with this practice, the stories are arranged in sections that focus on specific approaches and different perspectives that may aid you in this journey.

- **Section 1:**
  Cultivating the Ability and Skills to See Children
  Learn specific approaches and reflective questions to take up as you build your observation and documentation skills. Consider examples of stories that reflect the details of children's ideas and actions.

- **Section 2:**
  Planning Environments to Help You See Children
  Read stories about how to study children's engagement in early childhood environments, as well as consider suggestions about offering materials and experiences built on seeing how children use the environment.

- **Section 3:**
  Seeing Children with Others
  Strengthen your image of children's social skills and friendships. Examine yourself and how children see you.

- **Section 4:**
  Seeing Children and Theories of Development
  Study the details of children's experiences and how they are connected to theories and research about child development, the brain, and other learning theories. Explore how these findings can inform your practices with children.

- **Section 5:**
  Sharing the Stories of Seeing Children
  Read stories of teachers noticing the details of children's ideas and actions, the approaches they take to grow curriculum, and how they share what unfolds with children and others.

As you read the stories, take time to reflect on and marvel at the details you hear about children. Study the photos and think about how they provide you with more information, insight, and inspiration. Consider the ideas in the stories and how they can inform your own work with children. Remember that to really see takes time! Give yourself the gift of carving out the time for this important work.

Cultivating the Ability and Skills to See Children

- Seeing Children
- No Ordinary Moments: Using Observation with Toddlers to Invite Further Engagement
- Seeing Children's Lively Minds at Work
- Seeing Children's Ideas
- Changes in How We See Children

Throughout this section there are stories packed with observation details and descriptions of children engaged in everyday moments filled with extraordinary meaning. The secret to seeing children is to understand that most seemingly ordinary events have great significance if you stop to notice and study them.

As you read the stories, consider taking up the following:

- *Practice the skills of slowing down and looking for the details of children's intention and intelligence.*
- *Study the photographs and descriptions of children carefully to build your view of children's competence.*
- *Practice the observation skills reflected in the stories.*
- *Examine how photographs can capture children's actions and experiences, allowing you to see more deeply into the meaning of their work.*
- *Familiarize yourself with the Thinking Lens® protocol for reflection, study, and making meaning of observations and stories.*

Seeing Children

> *If we are not fully ourselves, truly in the present moment, we miss everything. When a child presents himself to you with his smile, if you are not really there—thinking about the future or the past, or preoccupied with other problems—then the child is not really there for you. The technique of being alive is to go back to yourself in order for the child to appear like a marvelous reality. Then you can see him smile and you can embrace him in your arms.*
>
> *~Thich Nhat Hanh*

The daily reality of working with a group of young children presents many demands for adults in early childhood programs. There are the ongoing chores of caretaking and cleaning up, planning and providing an engaging curriculum, communicating with families and coworkers, and the ever-growing pressures for outcomes, assessment, and documentation to prove that children are learning when they are with us. These pressures compete for our attention, making it difficult to keep the child at the center of our work. Most of us went to work with young children because we love their view of the world and wanted to share it with them. Yet, with all of these preoccupations and problems, how can we possibly stay truly present in the moment and really see children as Thich Nhat Hanh suggests above?

In my work with toddlers, I continually remind myself that although I may feel the challenges and pressures of regulations and outcomes, I am the one in the room with the children making decisions about what to pay attention to and how to respond. I essentially have the power in every moment, with every interaction, to be present and truly see children.

Learning to see children takes time and practice, both when I am with them, and when I take time to reflect on my work. The extra effort is worthwhile as it is much better to share in children's insatiable curiosity, deep feelings, and pure delight than it is to be the toddler police, focusing only on fixing behaviors, teaching to outcomes, or checking boxes on official forms. How useful or authentic are assessments without the child being fully present in them? To learn to see children and keep them at the center of my work, I have adopted the following practices as a regular part of my daily life.

Notice and Suspend Adult Agendas

It was lunchtime and I was very preoccupied rounding up the 10 one-year-olds I work with to get hands washed, bibs on, and everyone in chairs ready to eat. Through the chaos and noise I had been practicing suspending my adult agenda, even for just one second, to look closely and delight in the many moments unfolding before my eyes. I carry my camera in my pocket to record and revisit the moments when I have more time. When I saw Hannah looking at herself in the mirror, I snapped this photo.

In the midst of this busy lunch routine I was reminded of the deeper significance of my work. As I study the details of the photo, I can see that Hannah sees herself and this moment in her life as extraordinary. Her own image reflected back to her in the mirror brings her absolute pleasure. When was the last time you looked at yourself in the mirror this way? Can you remember why you stopped? If we still looked at ourselves and each other in this way it could transform how we live together.

We can only see through our own eyes, hear through our own ears, and relate to what is unfolding through our own experiences. It is mostly impossible to be objective as we walk around in our own skin, especially with all of the demands pulling on us. The most useful way to see outside ourselves and our adult agenda is to be aware of our own perspective as we relate to children and the daily challenges of our work. Once we are aware of it, we can choose to put our adult agenda aside to really see children. Doing this brings so much richness to our lives, inspires us to slow down, and enables us to truly acknowledge the children in our lives.

Study Photos to See More

With digital technology comes an abundance of opportunity to take photos. For a while, I was taking so many photos I didn't know what to do with them until I decided to use photos to tell stories of children and their work. While contemplating which photos to use for the stories, I discovered that if I studied them carefully, I could learn so much more about children's ideas and points of view.

I've since been re-focusing the photos to highlight aspects I want to see more clearly. I crop the photos by cutting out the background, and then enlarge the elements I want to emphasize. The example here of the two children outdoors exploring the hole helped me see the details of textures, shapes, and shadows the children appear to notice as they use their hands to explore. I understood more powerfully the appeal of the dark opening surrounding the utility cover, appearing as a mysterious, deep hole with the promise of a surprise if you reach inside.

I also crop photos to highlight what the children are doing with their hands or looking at with their eyes. I discovered that when I study their intent in this way it is impossible not to take what they do seriously. When you examine these elements, you can clearly see the intelligence, skill, and serious intent that children bring to their work.

Try Out What You See Children Doing

A few years ago, I discovered that I could learn to see children's perspectives in very powerful ways if I observed them closely and then tried out what they were doing. I had been frustrated with a group of boys who had taken to zooming small cars off of block ramps they built. They would fling the cars across the tilted ramps, watching them fly through the air, hitting the ceiling, the windows, and sometimes, people. I spent a lot of time trying to stop their behavior, but to no avail. After the boys left one day, my co-teacher and I decided to try out the cars and ramps ourselves. Much to our surprise, we had a blast! We experienced the excitement and challenge as we built the ramps and zoomed the cars. With this new perspective, we approached the children's work in a very different way. We offered the boys challenges to build their ramps more carefully and control the speed of the cars more accurately. They took up our suggestions and the activity became a focused, complex learning experience for all. Since then, trying out what children are doing has become a regular practice for me to see them more clearly.

Cropping can emphasize certian aspects of a photo and highlight what children are doing.

See Children's Strengths

As she got absorbed in her play, Wynsome dropped her binkie and forgot about it until she saw the one that T'Kai had in his mouth. She went up to him, yanked the binkie out of his mouth, and put it in her own mouth. T'Kai began to complain loudly. My first instinct was to launch into the conflict resolution techniques that I have learned over the years. Instead, I decided to practice seeing more details to help me find the deeper meaning underneath this incident.

After spending many days with these two children, I have come to understand that Wynsome and T'Kai share a strong connection around their binkies. They know firsthand how important binkies are and I think they associate their own feelings with each other. I've seen them offer a binkie

to each other when they are playing side by side. I also think that sometimes taking the binkie from the other is about trying to get closer by climbing inside each other's experience. It seems that Wynsome wants T'Kai's binkie rather than a binkie or her own binkie. Instead of seeing this incident as evidence that the children needed help with social skills, I see it as an indicator of their desire to develop a relationship.

With this in mind, I wanted to find a way for the children to work together. I invited T'Kai to go with me to find Wynsome's binkie so he could have his binkie back. T'Kai accepted this idea readily and we searched the play area together. When we found Wynsome's binkie, I suggested that we go to the sink to wash it off. Wynsome, listening to this exchange, eagerly joined us at the sink, bringing T'Kai's binkie with her so it could be washed too. Wynsome willingly gave the binkie back to T'Kai, and with the binkies in their rightful owners' mouths, the children spontaneously gave each other an exuberant hug. The children's eager participation with my suggestion showed me that I was on the right track. I marvel at their sweet connection with each other and see that sharing experiences is really what the children are looking for. I've discovered that my daily practice of seeing and taking action on behalf of children's strengths helps them live in their own competence.

Use a Thinking Lens®

To deepen the practice of seeing children, Margie Carter, Ann Pelo, and I developed what we call a *Thinking Lens® for Reflective Teaching.*[2] The lens, with questions for reflection, serves as a tool for utilizing the practices described here. Use the lens to notice your adult agendas, share in children's perspectives, and see their strengths. Slow down, observe, delight, and practice every day, for being with children in this way is not just a way of working, but a way of life.

A Thinking Lens® for Reflective Teaching

Knowing Yourself
How am I reacting to this situation and why?
What in my background and values is influencing my response to this situation and why?
What adult perspectives, i.e. standards, health and safety, time, goals are on my mind?

Examining the Physical/Social/Emotional Environment
How is the organization and use of the physical space and materials impacting this situation?
In what ways are the routines, adult behaviors, and language undermining or strengthening the children's ability to demonstrate their competence?
How could we strengthen relationships here?

Seeking the Child's Point of View
How do I understand the children's point of view in this situation?
What might the child be trying to accomplish?
What developmental themes, ideas, or theories might the child be exploring?

Finding the Details that Engage Your Heart and Mind
What details can I make visible to heighten the value of this experience?
Where do I see examples of children's strengths and competencies?
What is touching my heart and engaging my mind here?

Expanding Perspectives Through Collaboration and Research
What other perspectives could enhance my understanding of the meaning of this situation, i.e., perspectives of families, co-workers, colleagues?
How might issues of culture, family background, or popular media be influencing this situation?
What theoretical perspectives and child development principles could inform my understandings and actions?

Considering Opportunities and Possibilities for Next Steps
What values, philosophy, and goals do I want to influence my response?
How can I build on previous experiences of individuals and the group?
Which learning goals could be focused on here?
What action should I take from my teaching repertoire and why?

No Ordinary Moments:
Using Observations with Toddlers
to Invite Further Engagement

The year I spent closely observing toddlers as a child care teacher was one of the most intellectually engaging and joyful years of my career. I kept a daily journal and took lots of photos of the unfolding activities that seemed significant to me and the children. I studied the photos and notes for my own learning and also loved sharing them with children and their families.

Every observation was full of accounts of children's remarkable focus and determination, curiosity and delight. Whether happy or sad, angry or tired, the children brought to every encounter an innate optimism and an eagerness for new experiences. My observations confirmed the current research that reports that the natural inquisitiveness and drive of these very young children ensures that during the first three years of life their brains will develop faster than at any other time. With an astounding 250,000 brain connections growing each minute, there are no ordinary moments during this time of life. The significance of this work was humbling and exciting. My hope was to find a way to take in each of these extraordinary moments with children, to honor them, and help them grow.

Seeking Children's Perspectives

It took practice for me to slow down, look, and listen attentively; suspending any agenda I might have for what children should be doing. Instead, I tried to put myself in their shoes to understand the world from their point of view. Seeing the children's perspectives influenced my decisions and actions, and was critical for engaging with them in a deeper teaching and learning process.

Here is an entry from my observation journal illuminating the power of taking the children's point of view:

Today I brought in clear plastic containers with lids, packed with colorful, sparkly bracelets that I found at the thrift store. I immediately knew from my previous observations that these would be a great learning material for the group. As I observed the children, they were absorbed in using the materials just as I predicted. They loved exploring how the bracelets sparkled in the light from the glitter sealed inside. Of intense interest to them was fitting the plastic rings back into the cup and securing the lid. I'm always so intrigued by how serious toddlers are about this kind of work. Do they feel the satisfaction of conquering the challenge of a tricky puzzle, or soothed by the security of knowing that some things in the universe fit together just right?

Oscar immediately knew what the rings were for, and so he spent a very long time putting every bracelet he could get ahold of onto his arm. I was delighted that the other children seemed to understand the importance of this work to him and let him have many of their bracelets so he could complete the task.

At one point I noticed Kiran deliberately throwing the bracelets onto the floor in front of him. My initial reaction was to jump in and stop this behavior. One of my ongoing goals is to help the children see how to care for our materials. Fortunately, before I jumped in, I stopped to watch for just a moment. What I realized is that Kiran was purposefully throwing the rings. He had discovered that if he threw them just the right

way they would spin around and around like a top, until they slowly lost momentum and wobbled to a stop. I was thrilled to learn this new way to explore the bracelets and called the other children's attention to Kiran's idea. I'm so glad I stopped to see his perspective. I was astonished that he figured this out; he's only 14-months-old! His discovery is now a part of the learning games we play with the bracelets, and the children are getting quite good at controlling this small aspect of the science of physics.

Capturing the Details

Another observation skill I cultivated to enhance the teaching and learning process with my toddlers was to notice the many small things that occurred within the group. Children look closely at the details that adults take for granted and don't pay attention to anymore. We are quick to assign a label or meaning to what we see. General information such as "they loved playing with the water" doesn't give us much to engage with to deepen the teaching and learning process. Capturing the specific details of what you hear and see, documenting with a clipboard and pen, sketch, tape recorder, or camera can help you learn more about individual children and see the complexity of the unfolding moments. You also get ideas about additional things to offer to extend their interest for further learning.

Here's another journal entry where I used the details of what I was observing to help children connect with each other's ideas and actions:

I've been delighted to watch the changes in how my group of toddlers engage with the baby dolls and props in the room. For a long while they have been imitating the actions that come from their own experiences, earnestly trying to fit bottles in the dolls' mouths and cover them with blankets. As the children play with the babies I observe them closely to see what they do. I also love to make guesses about what they might be thinking as they play. I imitate their behavior and play alongside them. As they play, I describe the details I see unfolding around me:

"Kiran is feeding his baby a bottle."

"T'Kai is gently putting his baby to bed."

"Hannah is rocking her baby to sleep."

"My baby is crying. I'm going to give her a hug."

I notice that as I highlight their actions, the children seem to pay more attention to each other's play and often try what I have pointed out. I've been wondering if my comments may be helping their play skills grow.

Today I watched their behavior with the baby dolls change. The difference I discerned is the children were playing together with the babies. They watched and interacted with each other a lot more than usual. I am so curious about this new play. I know it is a stage in their development to start to play together, but it seems that broadcasting their actions has helped them make a leap in symbolic thought. Did watching each other pretend introduce them to the power of their imaginations?

I particularly noticed this with Oona's play today. The other children eagerly followed her lead as she fed the babies, wrapped them in a beautiful cloth, and rocked them for a long period of time. She noticed their attention to her and I think it enabled her to see herself and her actions in a new way. A dreamy look came into her eyes and a satisfied grin came over her face as she seemed, at that moment, to understand the power of her imagination. It was such a profound experience for me, witnessing her growing awareness of the magical world of make believe.

Using Observations with Children

As I continued to describe the details of my observations to the children, it was apparent that this had a positive influence on their play skills. I began to use my observations and photos with them more purposefully. My journal entries about our study of Flubber demonstrate the power of using observation stories and photos with children.

Flubber Journal Entry 1:

I invited the children to begin a study of Flubber today, which we will continue over an extended period of time. I have chosen Flubber because it is a substance that moves, flows, and responds to the children's actions. Today, as they worked with Flubber, I narrated their actions and pointed out things the children were doing to the other children.

"Oh look, when Kiran puts his finger in the Flubber he pokes a hole."

"Oona is using the comb to make dots and lines all over the Flubber."

"T'Kai is putting the lid on the cup."

I noticed as I described and pointed out these actions, the children seemed to copy what they saw and heard. They also stayed at the Flubber table a little bit longer than usual.

Flubber Journal Entry 2:
Today I brought a homemade binder full of photos I have taken of our Flubber explorations. I read the book to the children when they came to the Flubber table to play. They were engrossed in the story of themselves and the Flubber; and when I was done, a number of them looked through the book again. The children continued to explore the Flubber, trying out the tools and actions that were in the book. I continued to refer them to the photos and describe their actions. They stayed at the Flubber table even longer today.

Flubber Journal Entry 3:
I saw Wynsome sitting by herself looking at the Flubber book and she was imitating the poking action that Kiran was doing in the photo. She was poking the photo with her finger just like he was. I wonder if when she sees these reflections, she notices things not readily available when she is immersed in her actual experience with Flubber. When I reflect back children's work to them in these ways, does it help them develop a symbolic representation of it in their mind?

Flubber Journal Entry 4:
I worked with Oscar and Hannah with the Flubber again today using my observations and photos to show them back their work. As they played, I continued to describe what I saw them doing and pointed out their actions. After I had taken a number of photos, I immediately downloaded them into the computer, and invited the children to look at a "show" about their work. Many other children came over, fascinated to see themselves on the screen. They pointed excitedly, saying each other's names.

Oscar was very interested in seeing a photo of himself making an imprint in the Flubber with the edge of a plastic container. As he looked at the photo he made a grunting sound and pointed, indicating that he had pressed hard to make the imprint. I suggested that he show us with the real Flubber. This time as he pressed hard to make each imprint, he made the same grunting sound. Hannah showed us she caught on to Oscar's meaning right away. She demonstrated by pressing her hands together really hard and squinting her face as she made the same grunting sound. Both of them continued to make imprints in the Flubber grunting as they worked.

This thrilled me as I believe that the work we have been doing to revisit our actions with descriptions and photos has encouraged the children to create a shared language for the hard pressure needed for imprinting. I saw this event as important for the development of their symbolic thinking and language, but I also saw a bigger significance. I got to witness the miraculous process humans go through to develop language!

These few entries are just a glimpse of the joy and deep engagement that the children and I had together. Using observations and photos with children gave me a profound respect for their insights and abilities. Sharing these stories with the children's families helped us all slow down and appreciate this special time of life. What I discovered is that when I stopped, watched, and waited, I learned so much more about the children and myself. My actions communicated respect for the children, and in turn, furthered the possibilities for deeper meaning in ordinary moments. I came to trust the children as partners in the teaching and learning process. I couldn't wait to get to work each morning, looking forward to what the day would hold for us.

Recipe for Flubber

Mix in a bowl:
1 cup of Elmer's® glue
3/4 cup of water
Food color or watercolor

Mix in another bowl:
1/2 cup of water
1-2 teaspoons of Borax®

Pour both bowls into one bowl and mix.
Watch the magic!

Seeing Children's Lively Minds at Work

> *We overestimate children academically and underestimate them intellectually.*
>
> ~*Lilian Katz*

One of my worries about the growing focus on academics and school readiness in programs for young children is it keeps many teachers from seeing children's innate, lively minds at work. When teachers are overly concerned about teaching the alphabet and other isolated skills and facts, they may miss children's serious approaches to tasks and voracious quests to understand the world around them. As Lilian Katz's quote suggests, children are more apt to be interested in intellectual pursuits rather than academic lessons. I think clarifying the difference between the two can help teachers see and appreciate children's thinking, and in turn, offer meaningful experiences that engage their lively minds.

Webster's dictionary defines "academic" as "very learned but inexperienced in practical matters," "conforming to the tradition or rules of a school," and "a body of established opinion widely accepted as authoritative in a particular field." "Intellectual" is defined as "given to study, reflection, and speculation," and "engaged activity requiring the creative use of the intellect." Obviously, it is important for children to learn appropriate academic skills and tasks, but rather than overly focusing on these goals, I strongly claim and enjoy my responsibility to help children become engaged thinkers, excited about the wonders around them. Young children bring an eager disposition to learn all of the time, so it's my job to find ways to really see, appreciate, and further their intellectual pursuits.

Take Children's Actions Seriously

It's easy to dismiss children's explorations because they move quickly, make messes, and put themselves in seemingly risky situations. I have developed the practice of waiting before jumping into a situation to determine what the thinking might be underneath a child's behavior. I have come to see that with most everything children do they have something in mind; a purpose or question they are pursuing. When I take even their smallest actions seriously, I am astonished at children's deep engagement with the simple wonders around them; I notice they are studying and speculating, engrossed in the moment. Notice nine-month-old Maddie's lively mind at work in the following story.

Sounds and Sparkles

Maddie was captivated with the shiny, crinkly paper that she found in a basket. She grabbed the paper and began to shake it with excitement as it made a loud, crackling noise. Then she pinched it with her fingers and explored it with her mouth. She quickly began to shake the paper again. I was curious as she put the paper up to her eyes and then went back to shaking it. Was she noticing the light reflecting off the surface of the paper? Did she see the transparency of the paper?

Maddie's joy in her investigation was obvious as she smiled and laughed with me as she tried each new action. Her favorite activity was shaking the paper. I think she loved the sound she was able to produce and my reaction to her, and she may have been delighting in the sparkles she could see coming from the paper as it moved. Next, Maddie clasped the paper with both her hands and began to stretch and pull it, watching the paper intently as she did this. I wondered if she had discovered something about the paper when she was shaking it and was exploring it further with this new action. What noise will it make if I pull it? Does it still sparkle when I stretch it this way? I loved seeing the paper from her point of view and watching her joy and intense engagement with the magic of this unusual material.

Use a Thinking Lens®

I use questions from a *Thinking Lens®* that I developed with Margie Carter to help me to remember to slow down, look for the details of what is unfolding, suspend my teacher agenda, and try to see children's perspectives. As I participate with children in these daily quests for understanding, I document what I am seeing to tell the stories of their rich intellectual pursuits. I study my photos and notes carefully to capture the significance of the children's work. These stories show how children bring their whole selves—body, mind, and emotions—to every task. Notice the details and children's perspectives in the following photos and stories.

Immersed in Bubbles

Two-year-old Mackenzie was totally absorbed in an intense study of bubbles today. I watched her purposefully fill a small cup and then pour the sudsy, wet substance onto her hand. She studied her wet and soapy hand for a long while, and then poured some more water and bubbles on her hand again. I was surprised when, after investigating the bubbles this way for several minutes, Mackenzie leaned over and totally immersed her arms into the water, stretching her hands and fingers under the surface, and again looking closely at the bubbles on her skin. She spent about 30 minutes playing in the water tub this way.

I delighted in Mackenzie's rapt attention for this investigation. It was such a simple set of materials, but she found so much to investigate. Seeing Mackenzie's lively mind at work certainly counters the idea that two-year-olds don't have a very long attention span. I wonder what she was noticing as she gazed at the bubbles. Did she feel tiny sensations of bubbles popping on her skin and then try to see what she was feeling? Was she noticing light and color shining through the bubbles? Was she interested in the textures, sheen, and shapes of her hands and arms in the water? Whatever was on her mind, the intention and focus she brought to this work was obviously a serious intellectual pursuit.

Offer More to See More

When I see children exploring objects and materials with such concentration, I want to offer them expanded possibilities with similar experiences to deepen their investigations. I also want the opportunity myself to see more of what is on their minds and their growing understandings. Seeing toddlers' fascination with this magical substance called water, I decided to offer more ways for the group to continue with this intellectual pursuit.

The Magic of a Sponge

To build on the children's investigation of water, I offered them dry sponges at the water table. My hunch about their interest in this new material with the water was right on. The children approached the hard, dry sponges with great curiosity and intense exploration began. I loved the serious looks on their faces as they examined the sponges closely while they were still dry, and then quickly put them in the water. They manipulated the sponges, intently watching as they absorbed the water. The children discovered and then delighted in squeezing the water out of the sponges. They repeated the soaking and squeezing actions over and over again. Next, they became interested in filling the containers in the tub with water and the sponges. Oscar was determined to put every sponge into the container. Then he covered the sponges with water and watched the water and sponges spill

over the top. He repeated this several times. I think these experiences related to physics concepts, such as float and sink, absorption, and displacement. I am excited to learn more about the specifics of this learning domain, so I can offer the children more possibilities.

The children easily discovered how their actions had an impact on the sponges and the water. They eagerly learned from the materials, their own actions, and from watching each other. I was amazed at the children's attention and ability to take in so much information so quickly. They were just like the sponges, soaking everything up. Seeing the world through their eyes, I gained a new appreciation of just how amazing sponges can be!

Seek Multiple Perspectives

My interest in children's lively minds and intellectual pursuits led me to the book *What is a Scientist?* by Barbara Lehn.[3] It portrays the elements of inquiry for young children that are identified by the National Science Foundation. One of the elements of our *Thinking Lens*® suggests considering multiple perspectives to describe and understand the many ways to observe children naturally using these elements of inquiry in their explorations. This book helped me to see children's actions more complexly as I adapted the elements from it to use in analyzing and planning from my observations. Re-reading the observation stories above, can you see that even very young children are thinking and learning like scientists from the following list?

When young children think and learn like scientists they:

- wonder and ask questions.
- learn through their senses.
- observe closely and notice details.
- describe, draw, and write what they see and think.
- compare and sort by looking carefully.
- count and measure to make comparisons.
- experiment through trial and error and test predictions.

- keep trying over and over.
- work together with others and have fun!

These outcomes are also helpful when responding to concerns from parents and other professionals about what children are learning as they play. In the following story of four-year-old Joshua playing with colorful, translucent blocks you can see the lively mind of a scientist at work. Which of the science outcomes is he working on in his play?

Thinking and Learning Like a Scientist

One of Joshua's favorite places to work in our room is the Light and Color Table. Today he spent more than 35 minutes building, stacking, and knocking over the colorful, transparent blocks. He thoughtfully examined each piece before he added it to the line of blocks that he was creating. He lined each one end to end in a row, and then using his finger, he carefully knocked the blocks down one by one without disrupting the other blocks in the line. I was amazed at this difficult task he set for himself because it required much concentration and a steady hand.

It surprised me that Joshua didn't seem to be paying attention to the color or mirrored reflection, but instead to the size of the blocks. He put two long ones together and then two short ones, making this pattern each time. He chose the blocks carefully, putting the ones aside that did not fit his pattern.

He showed such diligence for this pursuit, because when he had mastered his goal with the blocks lined vertically, he switched to building horizontally across the mirror, and carefully knocked them down. I marveled at Joshua's attention for the physics of spatial relationships, gravity and motion, and the math skills he practiced while comparing and patterning with the blocks. It's remarkable how children discover and study these things for themselves in a richly provisioned environment, for we could never teach them all there is to know about these wonders in the world.

Engage with Children in Intellectual Pursuits

My work with children, even the youngest babies, is the most intellectually stimulating part of my life. As you read the observation stories here, along with descriptive details and the children's perspectives, you will notice that I make reference to my own interests, curiosities, surprises, and delights in what I am seeing. When teachers are intellectually engaged, side by side with the children in their pursuits, we see more clearly their lively minds at work, and respond in ways that enhance their identity as serious thinkers and learners. The following story is one of my favorites from my work with preschool children, as their joy and wonder about the magic of rainbows matched mine.

Catching Rainbows

In our room we have wonderful windows where on sunny mornings the light comes streaming in. Because our program is located in the often gray and rainy northwest of the United States, the sun is a welcomed friend. To celebrate the sunlight, we created a display in a window with prisms, mirrored balls, and hologram mobiles for the children to explore. The children eagerly gravitate toward the spinning lights and rainbows made by these items. They try out all kinds of actions on them to see what will happen.

The children think and care deeply about the magical colors and lights that visit our room. They are intensely curious and have formulated serious theories and questions about where rainbows come from and why they visit us. As they play with the light and rainbows through chase games and cause-and-effect explorations they are careful observers of important details. They clearly notice what is different on the rainbow days. A few have made the connection that when the sun is not out, the rainbows are gone. I delight in the theories the children share as together we seek deeper understandings of these amazing phenomena.

> *"The rainbow makes all of the colors in our room."*
> *"The rainbow comes from the clouds."*
> *"When it rains, the rain goes right through the rainbow."*
> *"Rainbows are colorful air."*
> *"The rainbow comes to visit because it likes us."*

The children's theories show what powerful observers they are of the scientific evidence at hand and also offer delightful interpretations from their unique perspectives. I don't interrupt these spontaneous musings for pre-planned academic activities. Nor have I researched an academic lesson about how rainbows are made. I know that embedded in their exuberant explorations are rich opportunities for collaborating, problem solving, hypothesizing, thinking, and learning. I don't want to limit the children's complex intellectual pursuits by focusing on teaching them the "right" answer.

My priority is for children's learning to include amazement, joy, magic, and wonder, rather than activities with no context and dry facts without meaning. I want them to "play" with their ideas about rainbows in their conversations and through meaningful activities. When the rainbows come, I delight with the children as they run and jump and chase the rainbows around the room. I suggest that the children think and learn like scientists by talking about and drawing their ideas and theories. I turn reflections into displays or books with photos and stories so the children and I can revisit their thinking to go deeper. After extensive exploration and study of their own theories, I offer books with scientific facts to enhance their discoveries. These are ways children experience meaningful academic learning.

I find that it takes daily practice for me to really see children. But I know that when I closely observe children's pursuits and take their ideas seriously, I see their lively minds at work, and how capable they truly are. When I join the children in their excitement about the world, I enrich my own life and work. Ultimately, when children are supported to pursue their interests and passions, they come to believe that their theories and intellectual pursuits have value. They experience themselves as competent thinkers and learners who can make choices about their learning. They learn to collaborate and see other perspectives and work through disagreements. They study something over time and in-depth to learn about it—in other words, they are intellectuals at work!

Seeing Children's Ideas

> *In the beginner's mind there are many possibilities. In the expert's there are few.*
>
> ~Suzuki Roshi

We offered our group of toddlers long, colorful, translucent tubes to enjoy and explore. As always, they amazed us with the many ideas they used to investigate and learn with them. The tubes are long and the children marveled at how they could easily lift these objects up taller than their bodies. The tubes also afforded them more reach as they eagerly stretched toward the sky and touched the highest boughs of the trees. The children discovered that the tubes are great for making sounds, both by singing into them and pounding them on the ground where they ring out a loud gong. They carried armloads of tubes around the yard, rolled them down the hill and slide, stuck them in the sand, and played peek-a-boo together;

looking through the long hole, as well as transforming the world with color. At the center of the children's explorations was their pleasure in sharing ideas.

I continually use the word "idea" and talk about its meaning with my group of 18- to 28-month-olds. When I observe them closely, I see that formulating and exploring ideas is central to these very young children's daily lives. They respond readily to the notion that they have an idea when I say things like, "You must have an idea about what you want to make happen with the…" "I see you have an idea you are trying." Children who are verbal have begun to use the word "idea" in their play as well as at home. I delight when I hear a child say, "I have an idea," and then proceed to demonstrate a new action. And the children eagerly take up the invitation to see and try out each other's ideas. In fact, describing one child's idea to another child and inviting them into the discussion often helps dissolve a conflict over a coveted toy before it erupts. It seems children are just as interested in each other's ideas as they are in their own.

Talking with children about their ideas should be a natural response to their enthusiastic quest to learn about the world. Yet so many adults are quick to react to the potential risk or conflict they think may occur when children explore ideas together. Of course, we have important responsibilities to keep children safe and to help them get along; but in our program, we believe that if we are truly to help children develop to their fullest potential, then our practices must support and extend the exploration of ideas rather than stop them.

Current research on brain development in young children supports what I see with our group: children have an innate drive to generate and explore ideas in order to learn. Researcher Alison Gopnik describes it this way:

> *"Babies are designed to learn—and this evolutionary story would say children are for learning, that's what they're for—we might expect that they would have really powerful learning mechanisms. And in fact, the baby's brain seems to be the most powerful learning computer on the planet."* [4]

I want to understand the implications of this brain research for my plans and interactions with these remarkable children. How do I grow my practices to "catch up" with the newest findings and the children's lively minds?

Observing Closely for Ideas

Seeing the significance of what toddlers do requires that I notice the small details that reflect the ideas going on beneath a child's actions. When I study their experiences, I see that almost everything they do has an important purpose or question—an idea they are pursuing. Cultivating my observation skills is the most useful way to begin to see, value, and extend children's ideas.

Responding with More Ideas

As we observe children's ideas, we come up with our own ideas in response. For example, picking up on their idea of exploring size and scale, my co-teacher Jesly and I offer different-sized materials in the sensory table so the children can try more ideas related to these concepts. In these photos Caitlin explores the idea of filling up a very large container with a very small one. It takes her extra effort to move the container to the ground where she can more easily accomplish her idea. We wonder how it must feel to her to be only a little taller than that container, and marvel at how she is able to lift it and dump the water back into the sensory table.

Helping Children Share Ideas

Because we see how children eagerly notice and try out each other's ideas, we try to provide more opportunities for this sharing to happen. How we set up the painting easel is a good example. We don't put names on a paper to give ownership to one painter or to keep children from painting on each other's work. We understand the children aren't yet attached to a product and instead delight in working together, moving around to the different sides of the easel, sharing space, paints, brushes, and ideas. We notice how keenly they watch each other's work and try out what they see. In this photo, Zane came across this painting of a yellow design that someone left to be discovered. We were amazed at how carefully he followed the yellow design, creating similar curves and lines with the blue paint.

Noticing and Planning for Children's Innate Ideas

As we observe children and make meaning of what we see, we discover that they often try the same ideas again and again. For example, toddlers seem to have a sacred quest to fill every hole or opening with an object, dump every container, mix and transform materials, follow a pathway, or make objects move down an incline. We have come to understand that repeated exploration of these ideas is inherent in children's developing brains and have discovered theories that support what we see. Piaget describes these repeated actions as *schemas*—a thread of thought that is demonstrated by repeated actions and patterns in children's play.[5] These repeated actions suggest that children's play is a reflection of deeper, internal, and specifically directed thoughts. When children are exploring schemas, they are building understandings of abstract ideas.

Because we have learned to spot and understand the ways children are exploring these innate ideas, we make sure we plan more ways for children to pursue them. For example, seeing that the children were working diligently to test how different objects rolled down the slide outdoors, we created another way for them to engage in a similar idea indoors with this invitation of ramps, balls, and spools.

Negotiating Your Ideas with the Children's Ideas

A group of our toddlers were engaged in water play outside that evolved into transporting cups of water from a large bucket and pouring them on the outside table. Transporting things from one place to another is one of those perfectly fine ideas that we see repeated again and again by children. At one point, two-year-old Kristina filled a cup to the brim and announced, "I have an idea!" She proceeded to walk indoors and poured the water all over the play dough table, turning the play dough into a goopy mess.

A huge part of our daily lives is negotiating children's ideas with our own. As I've worked to notice, respect, and extend children's ideas I often find myself in dilemmas such as this ordinary moment with Kristina. I am reminded about how much power I have in deciding whose idea has the most value and which ideas I'm willing to let unfold. It's critical that I clarify my thinking for myself, so in these moments I can remain flexible or have clear reasons to offer children as I respond to their differing ideas. Because Kristina knows ideas are important and respected in our room, her announcement gives me the chance to pause and see the logic in her idea, so I don't react from a belief that she is misbehaving.

I ask myself how often I stop an idea based on my logic, not understanding or misreading a child's ideas. Toddlers move fast, make messes, and often get themselves in risky situations as they pursue their ideas. Their brains work differently than mine. They see more, hear more, and experience more than I do. But I know that when I take even their smallest actions seriously, I am astonished by the children's deep engagement with simple ideas about the wonders around them. I marvel with them and learn from their ideas. They have so many more ideas than I do! In this demanding yet joyful process, I am learning to respond to the children with respect, support, and challenges that I hope will enable them to fully use their amazing capacity for ideas.

Changes in How We See Children

Which of these best describes how you see young children?

- *Children are inexperienced, vulnerable, and often get themselves into trouble; my first priority is their health and safety.*
- *Children say and do the darnedest things; they're so cute and funny and always keep me entertained!*
- *Children need me to help them develop skills that will get them ready for school and life.*
- *Children are eager, curious, creative, and competent learners, deserving of rich, challenging experiences to develop their fullest potential.*

All of these statements have simple truths to them. Yet, how we see children is not so simple. Our view of children and childhood is rapidly changing in response to the pressures of modern life, new research on brain development and learning, as well as the belief that many young children in the United States aren't ready for school. There are powerful messages coming from commercial, social, and political interests, as well as from many factions in our profession that suggest solutions.

"Early Learning Matters" is a slogan that reflects the changes in how our culture sees children, and many state and community initiatives for early childhood education have names like "Thrive by Five," "Best Beginnings," and "Project Liftoff." It's great that we have new resources and initiatives that show early learning is being taken seriously. However, within the promise of this good news are many challenges: How do these initiatives influence our view of children, and in turn, how do we plan for and respond to them within the context of our programs?

Outcomes focus on helping children succeed, and readiness and remediation are emphasized. Of course, we want to help children develop the skills to be successful in school, but does this focus narrow our view of children as people who need to be tested and fixed? Commercial interests respond with products and resources intended to guide us in helping children meet outcomes. While resources are useful for our work, it's important to question the view of children they suggest.

There is also increased attention to regulations and requirements to ensure that we are caring and educating children using best practices for health, safety, and optimal learning. Yet many programs respond by limiting the environment and activities offered to children. Do regulations and requirements impact our practices so much that we stop offering children appropriate challenges and rich experiences that contribute to their learning, their view of themselves, and life?

Reflecting in this way helps me realize that I need to continually negotiate these influences. How I see children strongly impacts everything I do and say in my daily work. I want to make sure I draw on additional sources to bring an enhanced view of children to my work.

Do We See Children as Scientists?

The writing of researcher Alison Gopnik has helped me understand and value the profound abilities of young children when they are able to use their flexible brains.[6] Gopnik promotes the idea that young children naturally bring the disposition and skills of a scientist to everything they do; this is how they learn and develop their brains. I want to notice and support children's innate ability to bring scientific inquiry to their everyday encounters as Gopnik describes. I want to offer them opportunities to engage deeply in the big work they are drawn to. This requires that I see children's competence and believe that their ideas are worth pursuing as the following story suggests.

The Hole Story

The excavation started when we decided to add heavy-duty, child-sized shovels to our sandbox. The children quickly discovered that these "real" shovels worked quite well to dig large holes and soon the sandbox became too small a space for this big work. The children decided to move the digging to the grass. Cutting through the sod with the shovels was difficult work, but the children were totally engrossed in this unearthing. The adults were initially worried: Would the holes be too deep and dangerous? Could the children be trusted to use the shovels safely? Many of the adults seemed unsettled with the children's voracious quest to keep digging deeper and wider. How far would they go?

Was this destructive behavior or an important way for the children to feel powerful and learn together? We decided to support the children's unstoppable interest and as the hole grew, so did the amazing collaborative learning.

The youngest children repeatedly used the shovels and buckets to dig, fill, dump, and fill again. For the older preschool children, the holes and dirt became a backdrop for big dramas, and the school-age children created a complex system of holes with connecting tunnels. Conversations expanded day after day with theory making about what might be at the end of the dirt: China, the other side of the earth, or the river that was just across the road.

When the weather changed, so did the children's work. Rain created wet dirt, which provided more opportunities to explore, make comparisons, discover, and learn. Dry, fine dirt created beautiful patterns in the sky as the children threw it up in the air and watched it fall. The cooperation and problem solving among the groups was more than we could ever have planned a curriculum around.

All along the way, the teachers had to negotiate our view of children and what we believed they were capable of and deserved. Observing the details of their work helped us know how to support their safety while allowing them to keep going. Although at times we struggled, we came to deeply understand the children's competence and trust in their ability to be engaged in multifaceted learning, with an incredible capacity to work together.

Ten years later, that dirt hole is still a source of vital connections and learning for children and adults. I can't imagine all we would have lost if we had stopped the children back then on behalf of protecting and teaching them.

Do We See Children as Spiritual Beings?

William Schafer suggests that children are born with three spiritual dimensions that we no longer experience as adults and that many people try to reclaim through spiritual practices such as prayer and meditation.[7] He describes these as:

Presence: Approaching life with pure awareness, free from internal judgment, comparison, fear, or desire.

Joy: A strong sense of being drawn toward something or someone in wonder, curiosity, and interest.

Awareness of others' awareness: The realization that we are not alone, and that others exist who are present to our experiences.

I have had many encounters with the spiritual dimensions that Schafer describes in my work with children as the following story depicts.

"I See You"

Snuggled together in the big stroller, my group of one-year-olds and I would head to the neighborhood park where there is plenty of space to explore and run in the grass. Located in the middle of the park is an interesting concrete structure that serves as a water park on summer days. Although I doubt it was designed for these young children, this structure was a magical world, wet or dry. The children were enchanted with the space as they moved through it, immersed in the experience. There are whimsical openings in the structure with different levels to look up, down, or through. The children delight in every detail: the shadows, shapes, textures, and different views from each hole, which provide endless opportunities to explore and wonder.

I was most fascinated with one game they invented together and played every day. At first I thought it was cute the way the children would play peek-a-boo, taking turns looking through the holes at each other and laughing uproariously together. But as I watched them day after day, I came to believe that something more profound was going on in that game.

The children radiated with feelings of joy each and every time they saw each other through the holes. Their elated laughter touched me in a way that is hard to express. I experienced what Schafer describes as the spiritual dimensions

of children: intense wonder in being present in these moments and being drawn to each other with pure joy in the realization that we see each other.

I now bring this experience to all my encounters with children in classrooms, airports, and stores. For instance, I will keep looking at a child, waiting until they notice me. The response I get each time is so very gratifying when we both fill with pleasure as we communicate the simple, yet powerful message "I see you." Try it for yourself. As you do, imagine how the world could be such a different place if we were all able to see each other in this way.

Do We See Children as Offering Us a More Meaningful Way to Live?

My view of children has been profoundly influenced by the educators of Reggio Emilia in their work promoting a strong image of the child. One of the most significant resources for me is the book *Reggio Tutta*.[8] It's a delightful, yet thoughtful guidebook to the city of Reggio Emilia, Italy, written by children. It is full of words, images, and drawings created by children to describe the city from their point of view. This book invites us to imagine how different the world might be if we really did take children's points of view seriously in the way we plan for our communities and how we live together in the world. I'm thrilled by this notion and try to imagine how considering children's views would impact the way we develop policy and design our communities: What changes would we make? How might the quality of our lives be different? The story of Music on the Bridge from London Bridge Children's Services in London, Ontario, Canada, gives a powerful glimpse into the possibilities.

Music on the Bridge

We have been working with children on a long-term project to study a local bridge in our community. As part of our investigations, the children engaged with the different sounds that they could make on the bridge. The children noticed that the deck of the bridge made a unique sound, since it was made of wood. They discovered that the metal supports on the top half of the bridge could be shaken to make a sound as well. The children loved to run on one side of the bridge and drag their sticks along the rungs of the railing.

A young mother, walking her small baby in a stroller, stopped to listen and watch the children. She leaned down to her baby and said, "Do you hear the music?" Many other people using the bridge paused to listen to the music the children were making as well.

The children's relationship with the bridge appeared to be connected to music. Making music on the bridge left the children feeling powerful and desiring to share this experience with others. As new children moved into the classroom, the other children shared their excitement, inspiring them to develop their own relationships with the bridge. Each day, the children asked to relive the experience, prompting us to make weekly trips to the bridge.

The children were eager to share this musical experience with people in the community. We collaborated with the children and made a plan to attach a sign to the bridge and put a can of sticks at each end, inviting people to explore music on the bridge. We requested people leave us a message about their experience. The response from the community was tremendous. We visited the bridge often to collect the comment cards from people who took us up on our invitation to make music. Here are some of the many comments the children received from their neighbors.

- What a great idea! The bridge music sounds fantastic.
- Thank you for a wonderful treat. It brought back memories from my childhood!
- I dragged the stick across the bars. I noticed that the sound got higher at either end. I wonder why? Thanks for the smile.
- Great idea. Try tying string or cloth around the stick to make different notes.

(continued)

- On my way to work I walk over this bridge. Thanks, children, for collecting sticks to make the bridge sing. I did it and walked the rest of the way to work with a smile on my face!
- I used to hate bridges before this. You make the world beautiful!

Comments like this from the public are a reflection of the value the community sees in the children's invitation. This initiative gave people the opportunity to view the children as members of their community who are capable and worthy of our attention and support. There was a true dialogue between the children and the community, as people shared suggestions and observations, offered praise, and raised questions with the children. The nature of this reciprocity has been generous and full of grace, bringing joy to people of all ages and backgrounds, and has helped to define, through this shared experience, our community.

Educators Lynda Dale, Kelly Caines, and Sylvia Curtis-Norcross

Now that you have read these stories, reflect again on how you see children. Consider the possibilities in the stories here or your own stories of the gifts children have offered you:

- *How will you change your view of children?*
- *How will your image of children impact your work?*
- *How can we all help others see the power and possibilities in children's points of view?*

Listen to the words of William Schafer here to deepen your reflections on these questions:

> *"Babies, by their very existence, call us back to something we all sense we have lost. They do not enchant us simply because they are 'cute,' but because they awaken in us a thirst that sleeps deep within some wellspring of yearning that we know we have neglected."* [9]

Planning Environments to Help You See Children

- Seeing Children Respond to Changes in the Environment
- Strategies for Enhancing Children's Use of the Environment
- Creating Invitations for Learning
- Seeing Children Do More with Less
- Seeing and Supporting Children's Rights to Choose
- What's the Risk of No Risk?

The most engaging environments and materials for children invite them to explore their growing interests and ideas, and to show us what they know. Organized, calm spaces that encourage children to initiate and sustain their own investigations gives teachers more time to slow down and observe what is unfolding. The stories in this section offer suggestions for creating environments that support both the children's and the teacher's work, as well as tools for studying children's involvement and enhancing the environment based on observations.

As you read the stories, consider taking up the following:

- *Study your own environment to see how it supports children's play and learning and your ability to slow down and observe.*
- *Try some of the suggestions for enhancing children's use of the environment and inviting involvement with Invitations for Learning.*
- *Consider your role in how children use the environment and materials. What materials do you offer? How much can children choose their own activities? What opportunities for risk and challenge do you support?*

Seeing Children Respond to Changes in the Environment

As a former member of a Design Collaborative for the San Francisco programs, Preschool for All and First Five, I had the wonderful task of working with teachers and family child care providers to study areas of their environments in order to make changes based on observations of children in the space, and the goals and values we had for providing engaging, complex experiences for children's learning.

Selina Chen had a group of very active four- and five-year-old boys enrolled in her family child care program. She was concerned about the boys' big body, rough-and-tumble play, and lack of focus in the small playroom where they spent a lot of time. To begin the change process, I offered the following questions to focus our attention as we observed the environment and the boys' activities.

- Where in the area do children work calmly, with focus for long periods of time?
- Where do the children seem to have difficulty focusing?
  - How is this area arranged?
  - What kinds of materials are in the area?
  - What specifically do children do with the materials?
- Where do children use their active bodies and large muscles in the environment?
  - What is the quality of their play in this area?
- How do children talk about the materials as they work?
- What kinds of interactions do children have with each other in each area?
- What role do adults play in each of these areas?

We observed this program several times over a number of weeks and discovered that the children played regularly, although for only short periods of time, with the small amount of blocks available. They rarely played with the other materials in this area. Instead, the boys ran around and wrestled with each other, engaging in mostly inappropriate activities given the small space. We determined that the lack of focus in the space could be due to overcrowding, the small number of blocks or other materials, and the predominance of plastic, primary-colored, closed-ended materials.

Experimenting with Change

I brought in some interesting loose parts and building materials and offered them to the children in a carefully organized way. We observed a huge difference in the attention the children had for these open-ended materials that were carefully arranged to invite their focus. The trays provided a frame for the materials, which defined a focused place to work. The variety of different sizes of wooden spools offered many open-ended possibilities for investigation, building, and learning. The large box with the lid also became a part of the play environment as the children used the lid as a ramp to roll the spools down and the box as a place to catch and hide them. The children immediately incorporated the loose parts and natural materials into their block building. They stayed focused on building for a long while, only stopping when it was time to go outside.

Selina and I scouted the Internet for photos of organized block areas with open-ended materials for inspiration. We discussed the principles we saw and how we might extend this kind of experience to the entire space. Together, and with input from the children, we made a plan for transforming this area into a well-provisioned construction zone.

Transforming the Space

Before we began the change process, we did a thorough assessment of what was available and how things were organized:

Before

- The shelves were overstocked with a variety of materials that didn't go together.
- There were dolls, blocks, manipulative toys, puppets, electronic toys, rattles, and other items for babies all in the same area.
- The materials were randomly stored on the shelves, making it difficult for children to see the possibilities for using them.

- Most of the toys were designed with limited purpose and were made of plastic, primary colors, which didn't foster complex investigation and play.
- There were posters reflecting a variety of topics all over the walls, creating a feeling of clutter and disorder.
- The small space was filled with materials, shelving, and a large bus, leaving little room to spread out and work.

We understood that these issues were all contributing to the children's rambunctious, unfocused play. We put our attention to designing the space primarily for building and construction. With the children's input, Selina chose to add a large set of unit blocks, tree blocks, and skyscraper blocks. I collected a variety of natural and open-ended materials that could be used for construction, design, and dramatic play in the area. We worked together to clear the space of all the toys and wall decor.

Starting with a clear pallet we created a calm, engaging space for the children by:

- using flat, open baskets to store materials on shelves so children can easily see what is available. Although we provided an abundance of materials, the shelves look organized and beautiful rather than cluttered.
- including a large selection of natural materials such as rocks, shells, and stones. The other open-ended materials were mostly made of wood and included items of different shapes, sizes, and heights.

After

- clearing space so there is plenty of room for children to spread out and do elaborate work on their own or in collaboration with others.
- storing blocks in large, open baskets, which makes it easier for children to see and sort through to find the different shapes. The baskets also make it easier for children to clean up.

Selina documented the children's work with the materials and created a display of photos with descriptions of the learning that happens through block play so parents can see its value. The children's work is also enhanced when they view the photos of their work on the wall and in a binder near the blocks.

Learning in the New Environment

The children have eagerly taken up the challenge of working with these new materials, and the complexity of their work is astonishing! We have seen the impact of the new space and materials on the children's learning in many different ways:

- **Initiative and persistence.** The design of the space including its size, the kinds and amounts of materials, and the serene, organized feel it has allows children the opportunity to spread out and do big thinking and big work. They remain engaged because the space helps them see what is available, and there are plenty of blocks and other materials to use. Children aren't interrupted in their thinking or actions to negotiate for enough room or materials to play with. This, in turn, helps them stay with their work for longer periods of time.

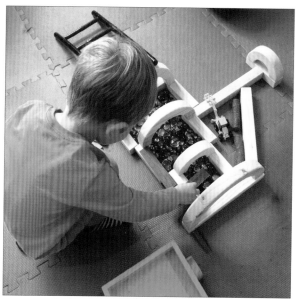

The children entered the block room with eager anticipation after weeks of conversations and decision making about the changes and additions they would find there. They responded with "ooh," "ah," and "wow" as they dove in to explore the intriguing new space and materials.

- **Math and science skills and concepts.** Loose parts, open-ended, and natural materials provide opportunities for children to use their flexible brains to explore classification, sorting, one-to-one correspondence, and other mathematical concepts. Children enjoy investigating and learning about objects from nature. They often use these materials to make careful designs, showing their innate affinity for the aesthetics of order and beauty in the world.

- **Meaningful literacy.** The books and other documentation included in the block area are related to architecture and design. The children immediately began to use these books to inform their block building. They "read" the photos and drawings in the books and transferred these images to re-represent them with the blocks. They practiced decoding symbols and developed their understanding that print has purpose and meaning. These are all critical skills for literacy development as well as problem solving.

- **Social skills and collaboration.** The large open space, with a multitude of interesting materials, provides the children with endless opportunities to share and negotiate new ideas. There isn't one right way to use the materials, so the children eagerly find ways to exchange ideas and work together!

- **The power of open-ended and natural materials.** Children's brains have what scientists call "plasticity"—they can actually see more, hear more, experience more, and feel more strongly than adults. With this comes the power to observe closely and see details. This gives children the gift of a fluid imagination and an ability to see multiple possibilities for objects and situations. In observing their play, we witness children's inventiveness with the loose parts and natural materials now available to them. These materials allow children to initiate their own theories, try out their ideas, and find solutions. They are amazing scientists, architects, and mathematicians at work.

Selina's Reflections on the Changes

The room for block play has been changed from a very colorful, busy, and crowded space, to a calm, natural, and focused place for children to play with blocks. The colors, textures, and theme are totally different now. Before, children were playing with different types of toys in this room, and some toys they didn't really pay attention to. After the change, they work together making buildings and bridges, exchanging ideas, staying focused, playing, and thinking for a long time. They are getting gentler with toys and respecting each other more.

I learned that the way we arrange the space and materials really impacts the children's focus. We can use simple and natural materials to create an environment for them to develop their creative thinking and let them explore and experience how things work. Also, I am amazed by how capable my preschool children are. I take the risk to offer marbles and small glass beads to them, and they handle these materials carefully, engaging and exploring them.

Strategies for Enhancing Children's Use of the Environment

Over this past year, many teachers have toured the wonderful room my co-teachers Rhonda Iten, Cindy Hayertz, and I have designed for the 16 three-to-five-year-old children we spend our days with. These visitors always mention how welcome and calm they feel in the homelike environment we have created. They notice the magic of the light, texture, color, and beauty they are surrounded by. They are drawn to the interesting, open-ended materials, and objects from nature.

These teachers have many questions as they look around our room. "How do you keep it so clean and organized?" "Do you let the children move things around?" "Don't the children break and lose things?" "What do you do about clean-up with so much available for the children's play?"

My initial answers to their questions have centered on the resources I have studied about early childhood environments. I have benefited so much from learning the approaches of the Creative Curriculum, HighScope, Montessori, and the beautiful environments of the schools of Reggio Emilia. Environmental experts Jim Greenman and Elizabeth Prescott have offered me much wisdom and practical advice. But as I reflect more on these practicing teachers' questions, I have come to realize that a rich and engaging environment for children requires more from us than a beautiful room arrangement.

Reflecting Our Values

Our strong belief in the value of cooperative play, big body activities, high drama, messy play, the sounds of childhood, working through conflict, and the importance of family involvement, all influence how we set up the environment. Our view of children as curious, competent, and capable of using and maintaining the beauty, order, and open-ended materials also strongly guides our room arrangement and the routines and activities we plan. Our emphasis is on offering rich childhood experiences where children can build their passions and attention over time, and use open-ended materials to create, rather than consume.

Children's lives today are filled with television, computer games, and toys that others have designed for them. They are continually entertained and directed, rather than challenged to create and invent for themselves.

Most children who come to our program don't start out knowing how to use our environment or the activities and materials very well. Rather than relying on us to externally motivate them with projects and activities we have planned for them, they benefit more from our intentional guidance and instruction to see the possibilities for their independent use of our environment.

Organizing Time and Routines

Once our room is carefully arranged, we plan for long periods of playtime. We want children to learn to initiate their own activities, use the materials and work with others for extended periods of time each day, and revisit their work day after day. We've come to realize this can't happen if we chop up their time into little blocks. We design our routines to include stretches of playtimes that are at least an hour. As the year progresses, the children are so engaged that they request longer times to complete their work.

During these times we allow the children's play to continue rather than requiring clean up and interrupting their focus. Because we want them to expand on their ideas, we encourage them to move things from one area to another if they can tell us their plan. One of the teacher's roles is to work behind the scenes recreating the order and beauty that will invite the children's involvement. We often leave the previous player's work as an example for the next child to build upon.

We provide ample time for clean up at the end of playtime. Everyone cleans up the entire room, which eliminates the cry of, "I don't have to clean up, I didn't play there." The children come to understand that we are all responsible for our room. During clean up, we emphasize how to care for the materials, and the importance of order and organization in helping us accomplish our ideas during playtime.

Clean-up time in our room is busy and noisy and takes a long time. We are very active in helping children stay involved. It has helped us to relax and let go of the idea that clean-up should be an orderly, quick, and quiet process. We know that we need to allow time and have patience and fun as we work with children on the important job of maintaining our wonderful environment.

Supporting Children's Play, Exploration, and Learning

There are many other important roles we have during playtime to enhance the children's use of the environment. Here are some glimpses of what you might see us doing.

- **Playing with children**—Children benefit when we model the use of materials and social skills for cooperative play. As we play with children, we focus on following their lead, and observing and assessing how to support and challenge them to go deeper in their thinking with the activities and each other.

- **Observing, broadcasting, and documenting**—As children play, we watch closely, take notes and photographs, and sometimes video and audiotape their activities and interactions. We use this documentation to show the children their ideas.

These have been powerful strategies for growing their use of the environment.

– As we play with children, we describe the details of what we see them doing in the moment. We also call the children's attention to what each of them is doing.

– We use the instant playback on our digital and video cameras to show and talk about what the children have just done.

– We create descriptive word and photo displays on the wall, in picture frames and notebooks, and put them in particular areas showing how children have used the materials in the past. We refer to these photos as sources of ideas and inspiration for children as they revisit the activities.

Helping Children Plan and Choose

When children enter the room each morning, we want them to understand that their job during preschool is to choose activities they will focus on while they are here. We have used a number of strategies to support them with this.

- **Planning board**—Adapting an idea from the HighScope Curriculum, we made a large bulletin board with photos of the activities available in the room. The children use the board each morning to decide where they will begin their playtime. We often put photos of the activities that the children have been involved with the previous days to remind them what they have been working on and suggest they continue in that area. As they decide, the children put their name in a pouch near the photo.

- **Planned activities**—We regularly create what we call Invitations to Learning. These are thoughtfully designed combinations and arrangements of materials that invite children in and suggest possible uses by how they are organized and displayed. We decide on these invitations through careful observation of the children's activities. For example, when we noticed children sticking toothpicks in the play dough to make designs and

sculptures, we created a beautiful display of other design materials (rocks, twigs, shells) for use at the dough and clay table.

- **Special interest areas**—When there has been an ongoing interest showing up in the children's play, we try to grow their involvement by creating an area in the room for further exploration and study. We display photos and previous work, and add new props and materials to keep the play going. As the children come in each morning, they eagerly look for what they had been working on the previous day. For example, after watching children use straws in the water table to blow objects around, we added new objects for expanded explorations of air over the next week. This grew into a long-term study of air pressure in a variety of forms.

Showing Children the Possibilities

We use our teacher planned and directed activities such as small group time and circle time to support children's use of our environment. We take these opportunities to demonstrate the use of materials and let children practice the skills they may need for accomplishing an idea during play time.

- **Teaching Times**—Adapted from ideas we learned from our colleague Tom Drummond, we regularly plan a time where we formally demonstrate the use of materials or tools. We do this in small and large groups. These demonstrations last from 5-20 minutes depending on the children's interest. We notice as the year goes by they last longer because the children are eager for more instruction. After the demonstration, children have the opportunity to explore the materials and tools for themselves. Some examples of what we demonstrate include:

– The variety of structures you can make with different shaped blocks.
– The many ways to use a paintbrush.
– The different lines and curves you can cut with scissors.
– The way to look at a flower so you can draw it.
– The possibilities for designing with pattern blocks.

• **Intentional Peer Group Experiences**—Ann Pelo, an amazing preschool teacher we know, shared with us the idea of "spicy work group time" to help children expand their possibilities for collaboration and play with others. We have adapted her idea and regularly have children who don't often choose each other as playmates work together. The children love the idea of "spicy" and come to understand that it means they might need to try a little harder to work things out with the other person. Offering this opportunity to children has expanded whom they choose to play with and has helped them learn what it takes to work things out when they have differences with a playmate.

The Invisible Structure

Our room has what might be called an invisible structure, which we see as necessary for children to use our environment with independence and complexity. We delight in watching children grow in their competence and claim their power. It's common for us to see children initiating their own activities in these many ways:

• Using every piece in the block area to construct an elaborate habitat for the animals.
• Painting a gorgeous collaborative mural.
• Making their own props from recycled materials for dramatic play.
• Creating elaborate designs with rocks, shells, and tiles.
• Designing intricate play-dough houses decorated with herbs and twigs for the plastic snakes.
• Inventing ramps, raceways, and point-tracking systems for high flying race car games.

- Drawing and writing to make a collaborative book about fairies.
- Exploring a multitude of ways to mold flour in the sensory table.

When we think of environments as more than room arrangements, but rather, encompassing a set of values, routines, materials, and interactions, the possibilities for children's learning and enjoyment are truly amazing.

Cristina and Krista's Amazing Habitat for the Animals

Every week, Krista and Cristina spend time working together in the block area with a variety of interesting loose parts available there. They create intricate block structures as a stage for their dramas and decorate them with the items available. Today, their play extended to almost two hours. They used every single item in the area to create a safe habitat for the plastic animals. They constructed an enclosure using hollow blocks, and then carefully arranged tiles, cardboard tubes, stones, carpet squares, and other materials in orderly rows and patterns. Next, they discussed which animals would go into each area of the structure. As they worked, their drama unfolded.

"This is a beautiful house to keep the animals safe from the storm."
"They need a sign to tell them where to come in."
"This is the place where they eat."
"Their house is very beautiful, they can stay in it a long time until the hurricane passes."
"Here comes the hurricane; quick, they have to get inside."
"The hurricane is here. They are safe."
"Pretend they really love their house because it is so beautiful."
"They want to live here forever."
"Yeah, they don't care if there is a storm forever."

We are astonished by the children's use of all the materials and the beautiful sense of design they bring to their creation. This is important work to them as they take a long time deciding on the placement of each item and animal in the house. Their discussion shows the pride they have in their work and the sense of order and safety they seem to feel as they complete this enormous project.

Creating Invitations for Learning

The birds living in a tree just outside the window of our school generated quite a stir among the three- and five-year-old children in our program. There was much excitement and delight as the children observed the birds build a nest and care for their new babies. To take advantage and expand on this wonder-filled event, I decided to gather some props and materials for our indoor environment and invite the children to more personally explore and represent what they were seeing through the window.

At the local craft store I found some beautiful bird families made from feathers, a set of tiny plastic eggs, and a few bird nests commercially made from twigs and feathers. I also collected feathers, dried leaves, grass, moss, and a variety of small, flat baskets. I carefully arranged these items on the top of a low shelf in the classroom and displayed books about birds and nests nearby. The children eagerly accepted this invitation, imitating the drama they had been observing out the window. They were especially drawn to acting out how the bird parents cared for their babies. The children also designed elaborate nests with the natural materials, sharing their theories about what kinds of nests the birds would like. Over the next month, the children continued to play with the birds and nests, poured over the books about them, and participated in many other activities and conversations sparked by this enchanting event in nature and the opportunity to pursue it in active, meaningful ways.

In my work as a preschool teacher, I have found that offering information about things that children have limited experience with, or posing a series of questions to try to encourage their thinking, doesn't seem to get much of a lively or sustained response. But when I carefully arrange props and representational materials in the environment with a particular focus in mind, the children are delighted to discover and play with them, eagerly share their ideas and theories, and seek more information. Because of this, I have been steadily collecting, organizing, arranging, and offering props and representational materials that captivate children's interest.

Designing Invitations

I call collections of interesting and carefully combined materials "Invitations" and I use them in a number of ways:

- **Invitations to respond to and enhance an emerging interest as with the Bird Invitation described above.** When I observe an interest among the group, I intentionally organize props and materials for children to revisit and represent their ideas. As I observe their conversations and activities, I get new information for what else to offer to extend the activities and learning possibilities.

- **Invitations to help children learn new skills and multiple uses for tools and materials that are a part of the daily environment.** I arrange materials and make displays throughout the regular areas of the room, often including documentation with diagrams, instructions, or photos of children's previous work in this area. For example, I arrange blocks and other block props in specific ways that suggest new possibilities for building and design and include photos of children's previous block constructions. The children use these Invitations as launching points for revisiting their work, adding complex ideas, and trying new skills.

- **Invitations to offer activities and experiences with particular content knowledge.** Designing Invitations related to math, science, social studies, literacy, and other content areas of early childhood education gives children experiences in wonderful ways that are engaging and natural for their active learning styles. When creating these Invitations I try to highlight a particular skill, concept, or information, and offer an engaging way to explore or practice the concepts. For example, I created a small sensory tub filled with lavender scented rice and included an array of hollow, plastic, three dimensional geometric shapes for children to fill with the rice. As the children work, they are exploring the physical knowledge related to geometric forms and spatial relationships. We name the words for the shapes as they are filling them—cube, cone, etc.

- **Invitations to introduce children to new concepts or events.**
  When I want to plan for a particular topic or concept, I arrange a collection of materials and props in an accessible place in the room for children to visit and use throughout the day. I observe their actions and record their conversations so I can uncover their ideas and understandings for further planning. For example, I assembled a display of dolls with different skin colors, photos, and books about the Civil Rights Movement and differences among people. I left them out a few weeks before the celebration of Dr. Martin Luther King's birthday. As the children interacted with the materials, I took note of what they seemed to know and understand about the life of Dr. King. I was surprised to discover how little the children knew about this great man, but also heartened to see their intense interest in his life and work around issues of fairness. The information and interactions spurred by this simple Invitation helped me design more meaningful activities around the holiday celebrations, based on the children's ideas and awareness.

Principles for Designing Invitations

As I have been studying how to collect and create Invitations, I have drawn inspiration from many sources. Maria Montessori and her well-known materials and methods, including Practical Life activities has made such an important contribution to my practice. Fredrick Froebel, known as the father of kindergarten, and the inventor of blocks, described his approach to organizing and offering materials as "gifts" for learning. The educators from the schools of Reggio Emilia, Italy, talk of "provocation" and have given us innovative ideas for the kinds of materials that engage children and careful, aesthetically beautiful ways to display them. I have also learned from many early childhood teachers and caregivers and their creative collections of Curriculum Prop Boxes. All of these sources are worth studying as you seek to enhance children's use and learning with materials in your environment.

The most important source for my learning about collecting and arranging Invitations in my child care room has been from the children themselves. When children are offered interesting open-ended materials, which are thoughtfully combined and arranged, you will see them work in amazing, yet predictable ways.

- **Exploring**—Children are drawn to the sensory aspect of materials.
  Principle: Look for collections that have textures, interesting surfaces for touching, looking at, or looking through, things that make sounds or move in interesting ways. Natural materials are always a good source for this kind of exploration.

- **Transforming**—Children are completely mesmerized with transforming materials and rearranging the world around them.
  Principle: Look for materials and substances that can be changed, moved, reconfigured, or otherwise have some kind of cause-and-effect quality.

- **Organizing and Designing**—With an interesting, varied collection of materials, preschool children will organize them by their attributes or use them in beautiful designs.
  Principle: Find collections of materials that have similarities and differences, and can be used for sorting, patterning, and designing.

- **Building and Constructing**—Young children like to put things together in relationship to each other, to connect things to other things, and to use building and construction materials to represent many aspects of their ideas and understandings.
  Principle: Along with typical early childhood construction materials, seek out interesting shapes and sizes of items for building, as well as things that can be used to decorate constructions. I also look for loose parts and recycled materials that resemble parts of something else, such as an airplane wing, a boat shape, or a dinosaur's scales.

- **Dramatizing**—With limited props, preschool-age children will turn anything into dramatic play.
  Principle: Keep an eye out for props and figures that can be added to any of the above background materials for an adventure or story.

- **Drawing**—Drawing is a natural medium for young children to express their ideas.
  Principle: Regularly provide tools for children to draw and write as a part of Invitations.

- **Reading**—Children will thoughtfully study books and visual information related to a collection of props they have been using for exploring and representing.
  Principle: Include resource books, stories, photos, posters, diagrams, and instructions to enrich the use of the materials by offering new suggestions and extensions, and support the development of literacy skills.

Collecting, Arranging, and Displaying Invitations

The set of materials I gather depends on the focus of the Invitation I am creating. I always make sure that the collection has at least three or four aspects from the list above so the children will have a variety of options for combining and using the materials. I am always searching for items that convey a sense of magic and wonder, treasures that beg to be a part of a drama or creation, as well as those that are substantial and have an important aspect or function. For example, in an Invitation to explore stones, I gathered a set of identical stones of varying sizes that are smooth and heavy to touch; they can be seriated by size, balanced and stacked into a tower, or designed as a habitat for a drama using a family of plastic snakes. Included with the collection are books about designs in nature, rocks, and snakes.

I have found that the way materials and props are offered is as critical to their use as the materials themselves. Thoughtfully collected and carefully placed materials help children focus on what is available and spark their ideas and actions. When arranging the display, it is important to position the materials in an orderly fashion so children can see what is available and the possibilities for their use.

- Designate an accessible location with enough space for one to four children to work with the Invitation, such as a low shelf, counter top, or small table. If I'm creating an Invitation in a regular area of the room, I make sure it is out of the way of the typical use and traffic flow.

- Provide a background for the materials such as a cloth or a tray to highlight the materials and define the work area. I think of this as offering figure/ground support like a puzzle, or a blank artist's palette to invite the work that will be done.

- Offer collections of like objects, for example all metal tools in the sensory table, all wood containers for sorting, or all natural baskets for storage. These like objects create a context for the materials so the Invitation does not look cluttered.

- Place like objects in baskets near the tools and materials that can be used so children can see what is available and how the materials relate to each other.

- Arrange the materials in beautiful ways that suggest how they might be used. For example, design a beginning pattern with tiles, partially build a small construction, offer an example of a simple drawing done with colored pencils, place the correct number of beads in the section of a tray with the corresponding numeral.

Scouting for Invitations

Once you begin providing interesting open-ended materials and observe the marvelous ways children use them, you will be eager to search for and provide more. Always be on the lookout in thrift stores, craft stores, garden shops, and garage and estate sales. You can develop an eye for the perfect treasure based on what you have seen children do with similar materials. You can also take a chance and offer children something that jumps out and captures your own curiosity. It's always delightful and surprising to see children's unique ideas and approaches. What better way to offer learning experiences—as an Invitation to wonder, explore, and create in as many ways as possible!

Seeing Children Do More with Less

Imagine not offering babies any toys until they find their hands for play. My mind started spinning as I heard Janet Gonzalez-Mena describe this approach used by the Pikler Institute in Budapest, Hungary, where they have documented over 75 ways that babies learn to use their hands for play.

This is such a different emphasis than what I often see in early childhood programs and homes in the United States. Babies are regularly surrounded by colors and images on walls and fabrics, along with toys that beep, rattle, and flash. Older children are presented with a multitude of toys and materials, together with activities planned and led by teachers and parents. I share some of this emphasis, as one of my favorite things to do is to design and create environments for children. I love to find and offer interesting materials for children's exploration and learning. I have a wonderful collection of open-ended materials that I present as Invitations, and I always look forward to what children do with what I offer. Although I am always thoughtful to avoid over-stimulation, as well as to ensure the materials encourage children to be the inventors of their work, the story of the Pikler babies and their hands challenged me to rethink my practice. What might be the impact of these different approaches on the development of children's creativity, initiative, and self-regulation? In my desire to give children all they need to grow and learn, am I giving them too much?

Look to Children to Learn

I always turn to children to be my teachers when I come up against new ideas and challenges. And, indeed, observing closely and reflecting on how children engage in exploration and discovery reinforced the notion that children, in fact, do more with less as the following stories illustrate.

Boxes and Babies

Fourteen-month-old Rosa is sitting on the carpet surrounded by a multitude of interesting boxes that I've offered this group of babies in the child care center I'm visiting. She knows better than me, as she scoots herself away from the big pile and finds one box with an attached lid to explore. I watch her work for 20 minutes on the many strategies she can find to open and close the box. She struggles with her motor control, but that doesn't stop her. I wonder why she isn't frustrated, as she never quite gets the lid all the way open. She lifts and watches as the lid falls back in place. She listens to the sound it makes as it closes. She holds onto the lid and shakes the box. I barge in and show her how to open it all the way. She wisely ignores me and goes back to her work, partially lifting, watching, shaking, and listening again. I get bored with her exploration of this box, so I get another one and offer it to her. She ignores me again and goes back to her work. I think, "Okay, what's so interesting about this box?" I lean in to get closer to her experience and that's when I notice what she has already discovered: there is a slight gust of wind that hits our faces as the lid falls to close!

More with Boxes

My long-time friend and co-worker Rhonda is visiting me with her five-year-old son Finn. I always make sure I have some interesting materials to offer him when he visits. Today I present him with two beautiful piles of tile and wood pieces. He eagerly plays with these for about 10 minutes, until he notices the large, flat cardboard box in my hallway waiting to be recycled. I'm a bit disappointed because I was so excited to give him the beautiful materials. But then I observe him for the next hour as he is immersed in play with this box. He plays on top of the box. It's a surfboard and a bridge. He stands it up on one side and it becomes a barrier to storm through.

He finds different ways to open the box and keep it open, which is no easy task because he has no tape. He invents a game of popping out and going back in the box and plays with this idea over and over again. He gets inside and we hear his dramatic conversations with the imaginary characters that are visiting him in there. At one point he asks for some markers; and then the box becomes his pallet for drawing, writing his name, and then a backdrop for another elaborate drama that unfolds as he draws.

A Simple Patch of Grass

This is our space. It measures about 40 feet by 40 feet. A chain link fence on three sides and a brick wall on the fourth side define the boundaries. Our space has a maple tree in one corner with a tiny garden that we created a few years back. There is a stone walkway that leads from the gate to the front door and there are three small benches made of cut logs. This space on its own, without the presence of children, seems cold and barren. The grass is patchy, the ground uneven and mucky. But an amazing thing happened when we added a group of toddlers to the space—they breathed new life into it!

We began to notice that the toddlers were finding things—items that we couldn't even see; things we didn't even know existed in that space until the children brought them to us. We found sticks, maple seed pods, pebbles, and leaves. The toddlers used the items as props in their play, and also as tools to further their exploration. Strange things began to happen. The toddlers didn't ask us for toys when we went into the yard; they were almost silent at times as they picked at the earth or busily collected items. They seemed to be working more collaboratively in this space than they were indoors, and they were surprising us with their resourcefulness—one of our two-year-olds resolved to put a small rock on top of her pile of leaves to prevent them from blowing away! We found bugs, snails, and worms, and the toddlers quickly developed a great respect for these living creatures. I am absolutely awe-struck each day when we take our toddlers out to this space. The effect that the space has on their moods, behaviors, reactions, and cognitive processes is incredible!

Shelly Brandon
Toddler Educator,
London Bridge Childcare Services,
London, Ontario Canada

The Flexible Brain

Researcher Alison Gopnik in her book *The Philosophical Baby* describes the amazing flexibility of young children's brains.[10] She says humans are born with an undeveloped prefrontal cortex, which is the part of the brain that helps us block out stimulus so we can focus on a task. We often characterize children's shifting focus as a lack of attention span, when in fact, what is really happening is they have attention for everything. Because children haven't yet developed the ability to block out stimulus, they actually have the capacity to hear more, see more, and experience more than adults do.

You can certainly see this at work in Rosa's investigation of the box. My limited focus was on the task of opening the lid. Rosa's interest was in the many possibilities that the box offered for her exploration, including the breeze she discovered she could create with her actions. My narrow ability to see the many possibilities in that one box as Rosa did, prompted me to interrupt her ingenious explorations. Luckily, at this point in her young life, she has the disposition to stay with her interests, and use her amazing brain the way it was intended. How long will Rosa and other children we work with continue to pursue their innate interests and abilities if adults like me interrupt their explorations with suggestions and offerings of more and more things to distract them?

Self-Regulation and Initiative

Current research in our professional literature, and many recent reports and articles in the news suggest that Finn has developed initiative and self-regulation. According to Hyson, some of the characteristics of children with these skills are:

- Shows curiosity, eagerness, and motivation to learn.
- Identifies and clearly communicates what he wants.
- Delays gratification and has tolerance for frustration.
- Persists at a task with an ability to focus and sustain his attention.
- Reasons, plans, and uses flexible methods for problem solving.[11]

Studies show that children who build initiative and self-regulation skills have more success in school and life. In fact, some say that self-regulation is as important to success as a child's economic background.[12] This research causes me to squint my eyes and think about my practice: What do I do that may impact children's opportunity to develop these skills?

- Do I offer too many materials?
- Do I jump in too quickly?
- Do I plan too many things for children to do, leaving them with little time to develop their internal resources?

I think we sometimes have the idea that self-regulation comes from getting children to follow the rules and routines, and to sit still and listen. We spend a lot of time on behavior and group management skills where we use rewards such as stickers or special privileges or punishments like time-out. We plan almost all of the activities and offer materials invented by others on behalf of helping children focus and learn. Yet these are all examples of externally driven strategies that may distract and deter children from their natural eagerness to learn and motivation to be competent, contributing members of our group.

Supporting children in developing self-regulation isn't an easy task in our complex world and work. I continually remind myself of the importance of slowing down to really see children as I discovered in the following story.

Block Dance

A number of years ago I was confronted with my restricted point of view when I was consulting in a program that had very limited resources and few materials for children to play with. The program I worked for had funding to help the teachers assess their environment and order more materials to enrich the children's experience. Before the addition of the new materials, I had the pleasure of observing these children do so very much with so little.

The children had access to an open, carpeted area with a small collection of cardboard blocks. One afternoon, as the children woke up from their naps, one by one they slowly took the blocks off the shelf and began to play, until there were nine children negotiating this very small space and small collection of blocks. One of the children built a simple tower adding blocks until it got tippy and fell over. Another child noticed the blocks that had fallen and picked up some of them to use in her tower. She, too, built a structure that eventually fell over. Another child who was working nearby saw the blocks and took some to add to her building. In another corner, a couple of children were connecting five or six blocks together, taking turns, continually rearranging the blocks over and over in harmony and simplicity, but always differently.

I was stunned! There were no outcries when blocks were taken. No complaints about not having enough. No lack of ideas to explore. The children were engaged in a graceful dance of give and take, using this limited supply of blocks in remarkable ways. I witnessed these kinds of gracious interactions among the children during many visits to this program.

At some point the teachers and I worked together to order more materials. When I eagerly arrived to see how things were going with the new things, I discovered the teachers hadn't put any of the new materials out yet. They were still wrapped in plastic in the cupboards. I suggested we take a variety of things out for the children to explore. I was shocked when offering these new materials provoked very different behavior in the children. This time, even though there were plenty of materials, rather than their usual collaborative play, there was conflict. Children vied for their turns and took things from each other. There were loud complaints and hurt feelings.

As I reflect back on this experience, I wonder if offering children less leads them to invent more cooperative, innovative ways to work together. Does abundance breed greed? Does simplicity grow generosity? This certainly was the case with this group of children.

In our consumer-driven, capitalist society there are many interests competing for what we use in our work with children. Much of what is offered is very seductive. We all want the latest materials, curriculum, or techniques to ensure we give our children all that they deserve. Yet, I want to be cautious and look for inspiration from children, places such as the Pikler Institute, and from other teachers like Shelly Brandon whose preceding story of a patch of grass is such a great reminder of the importance of slowing down and delighting with children in the ordinary places we spend our days. Her story reminds us that we as teachers can do so much more with less, just like children do.

Seeing and Supporting Children's Rights to Choose

By Deb Curtis and Jess Guiney

Willa's Morning

When I come to school, I can do all the things I like to do. It's true! At my school, there is a yard, and different rooms, and most of the time I can go wherever I want. In the morning, there are meetings with the teachers and the other kids. I have to go to those, but I get to share with everyone what I plan to do with my day. Then I go quick as I can to do my plan! Some days I want to go to the studio where

I can do any kind of art. There is a teacher there who helps me find what I need, and there is lots of space to work. There are other kids there, too! Sometimes we work together; other times I work by myself. I can stay as long as I like. The teacher helps me learn new things like how to use clay and how to paint with special paints and brushes. And, if I decide that I want to go somewhere else but I'm not finished with my work, I can come back and finish it later. I can go to any of the other rooms when I want to. I can even go outside, without having to ask! At my school, I get to choose who I want to play with, too. If my friends want to play all day long in the yard, we can. Even if it's raining! Or, if we want to make airplanes everyday, and then bring them into the block room to build an airport, we can do that too. At my school, we can do anything! So I always choose to do the things that I like best.

Javier's Morning

When Mama brings me to school today it is circle time. My teacher points to a place on the carpet where she wants me to sit. I go there, but I would rather sit next to my friend Marcus. He is bouncing up and down on his bottom and that looks like fun, but the teacher tells him to sit still. I feel like rolling around on my spot because Marcus thinks I'm funny, but the teacher tells me to sit up straight.

The teacher is pointing to something on the wall and talking about the sound it makes. This isn't much fun, so I'm really glad when she says it's time to go to the gym. She holds up a big poster with pictures and words. She tells us it says to walk in a straight line and put one of our fingers on our lips so we don't talk. She says our other arm should be stuck to our side. Then we are supposed to line up and sit against the wall of the gym. There are some big wooden boxes and benches to climb on in the gym and I can't wait to play. But the teacher tells us we have to wait for each of the children in the front of the line to take their turn running and jumping. I am excited as I watch the other children and I jump up and down, but my teacher keeps telling me to sit down. Finally it is my turn and I run really, really fast. My teacher is yelling at me to slow down, but I don't even fall. When I'm done I have to sit and watch again, so I'm glad when it's time to go back to our room. I really want to play in the blocks today with Marcus, but my teacher tells me it's my day to go to the painting easel. I like to paint, but I really want to play with Marcus. I hope he gets to paint with me.

Differences in the Right to Choose

Look at the contrast between Willa's and Javier's descriptions of their time in their early childhood programs! At the heart of their experiences is the right to choose. There is not much conversation in our profession about children's rights when it comes to how children spend their time in our programs. With good intentions we plan environments, routines, and experiences for children around what we believe they will enjoy and benefit from. If we have a child-centered philosophy we may have times during the day where we offer choices, but this doesn't mean we think that children have the right to decide how they spend their time. And we may not consider the impact that expanding or limiting these rights has on their lives.

Willa exuberantly claims her right to choose how she will spend her day and with whom she will spend it, while Javier's limited rights result

in reprimands for the few choices he attempts. Most early childhood programs probably fall on a continuum somewhere between these two very different scenarios. It seems important to us to examine the possible impact of these differences in children's right to choose on children's experiences, development, and learning.

Initiative and Self-regulation

We can imagine that a child presented with opportunities like the ones Willa described would probably excel in her ability to make good choices: she is allowed to practice constantly! When given the right to choose, children can develop real initiative. Willa:

- describes a teacher in the studio who will provide the materials she asks for.
- learns that she can request—and will receive—what she needs to put her plans into action.
- gains intimate knowledge of the materials that she chooses to use because she has the time to fully explore without interruptions and an adult who supports her growing interest and ability.
- is free to make a mess—or maybe a mistake—knowing she'll have the chance to return to her work to add more ideas, to clean up the mess, or fix her mistake.

Javier describes experiences in which he rarely has the right to choose. The goals set for him seem to be to learn to follow directions. Many people have the mistaken idea that getting children to sit and listen to directions is how they will develop self-control. With Javier this approach sounds like it will be a struggle. Because he is told explicitly how to approach each part of his day—from where to sit and how to run to what activity he may participate in—he doesn't have the chance to learn to make choices for himself. At the easel, he probably won't have the opportunity to explore the paint with his hands, or to freely mix colors. He may not really attend to the paints at all, instead focusing on how much he'd prefer to be playing with Marcus.

There is a lot of attention and research on how children develop initiative and self-regulation as critical goals for early childhood. In her book, *Mind in the Making*, Ellen Galinsky identifies seven life skills that include children being able to make choices, control their own behavior, and sustain their attention for significant periods of time.[13] We can see in the descriptions of Willa and Javier's experiences that having the right to choose promotes these skills, whereas limiting children's choices and directing them externally undermines initiative and self-control.

Eagerness to Learn

In our scenarios, the voice of each child suggests that their views of themselves differ too. If we consider Alison Gopnik's work on brain development in young children, we know that children have an innate eagerness and immense capacity for learning.[14] Willa is able to live out her natural disposition to explore and experiment using her right to choose. She sounds exuberant, confident, and certain of herself. A child in a program like hers would probably feel like masters of their own fate, and would have a pretty reasonable sense of their abilities, since they would be able to regularly test them.

Javier brings this same eagerness to the interests he expresses. He also is ready to take up his right to choose. Yet, when his teacher opposes his desires and regularly corrects him, he might begin to wonder if taking the initiative is somehow "wrong." It seems possible that this could adversely affect his behavior. As a result, his eagerness to pursue his own ideas might diminish and he may feel the need to test limits to discover just what is acceptable and what isn't.

Social Connections and Learning

There is a lot of joy in Willa's voice. It sounds like she enjoys her time in her early childhood program. It seems reasonable to assume that most of her peers would too; they engineer their own days. They have the time to fully explore their environment and build relationships with peers and teachers. Unfortunately, it sounds as though Javier doesn't even get to choose who he plays with. It's difficult to learn how to relate to others if all of your interactions are structured. Honestly, he doesn't sound too happy, and one might guess that his teacher isn't happy either if she feels she has to spend most of her time herding children from one activity to another.

Vygotsky's learning theories about social constructivism support the ideas that: 1) Children learn in relationship with others; 2) Being able to fully engage with like-minded friends can scaffold children's development more readily than can teacher-directed activities.[15] Both Willa and Javier are excited to engage with their peers, but we can see again the advantage Willa has in being permitted to pursue significant friendships of her choosing. It takes time and shared experiences for children to benefit from the bonds and scaffolding that these friendships provide.

Rights and Responsibilities

One might wonder why a program like Willa's doesn't end up with a bunch of children running around crazily and aimlessly.

- If children have the right to make choices about their time and activities, what skills and knowledge do they need to choose well?
- How do we support children in making responsible choices so they can practice the critical dispositions of initiative and self-regulation, and sustain their eagerness and joy for relationships and learning?

Believe Children are Capable and Deserving

Our view of children strongly determines if we support and challenge them or direct and correct them. Adults must believe that children deserve the right to choose and are capable of understanding that with rights comes responsibilities. If we believe this, then we will use our role to coach children in making good choices.

Organize the Environment

A teacher who values autonomy in decision making will organize the classroom so that materials are accessible to children and that children are responsible for the care of those materials. Children benefit from an environment that is intentionally designed and well provisioned with engaging materials so they are able to see what is available. The arrangement and care of the environment communicates to children the value of focus, collaboration, and choices for complex play and learning.

Support Children

Since teachers in programs like Willa's don't need to spend their time directing children, they have the opportunity to work beside children, supporting them as they learn to make productive decisions about how they spend their time. They take time to observe children's play, introduce relevant materials, support particular interests, and scaffold learning.

- A teacher who is tuned in to the culture of the classroom has the opportunity to suggest possibilities and to help children sustain their focus:
  - *"I notice that Emma is using the hollow blocks to build a tall tower. I saw you do that last week. Maybe you can try together."*

- Teachers also can document and share the stories of children's complex play and relationships. They help children see responsible choices by describing and displaying photos and homemade books of focused, cooperative play.

- Teachers can reinforce responsible behavior when issues arise:
  - *"Tearing the books damages our learning materials. Let's fix this book, so all of us will be able to read it."*

Assess Your Program

As you work to build a program that ensures children's rights to choose:

- examine your daily schedule and routines.
- record the time periods for all of the activities and transitions that occur throughout the day:
  - How often and for how much time are children choosing what they will do?

- How does the physical environment support children's choices? Is it organized and orderly, and does it offer interesting possibilities for children's engagement?
- what is the quality of the choices children make?
  - Are children able to initiate and sustain their attention in interesting projects with others for significant amounts of time?
- how do you support children in making responsible choices?
  - What might you do to provide more time, coaching, and opportunities to honor children's right to choose?

River Room Musicians
By Karen Golosman, The Learning Center

A small group of girls came together on the red couch to create a performance area. They placed long wooden blocks under their feet and gathered rain sticks and wooden ramps to use as violins. They explained that the orchestra would start when they pushed their feet down on the blocks and the music would begin when they played their violins together.

When I saw them playing, I asked if they would like some real violin music to accompany them. With their positive response, I turned on the CD player. The girls began playing in unison again, in time to the violin music they heard. Their faces were filled with joy, inviting other children's curiosity. One by one, new musicians joined the orchestra. Then Cassie decided the group needed

a conductor. This "symphony" was a wonderful collaboration by the children. It was amazing to see how they held their "instruments" and kept in time with the music! The concert continued for a long while until Ansel jumped up and declared, "I want to play the guitar!" He transformed his violin into an air guitar. The other children followed his idea, jumping up and changing the tempo of their playing. Ansel told me, "We need rock and roll music!" It was wonderful to see the children think "outside the box" and find such a unique use for everyday materials.

Outcomes

The preceding story is a simple, yet remarkable example of what can happen when children live in an engaging environment where they have the right to explore and develop their own ideas, and to share and collaborate with others. The children in this classroom have many interesting materials to choose from, the time, and support to develop skills for thinking creatively and working together.

We see in this story that the children readily took the initiative and used unique materials to invent and play the violins. They easily accepted new members into the orchestra, showing they enjoyed collaborating and sharing the stage with others. They eagerly followed each other's ideas.

We believe when children have the right to choose in these ways and are helped to be aware of their rights, they learn to advocate for themselves—and will learn to advocate for the rights of others. Consider the implications that developing this social responsibility at such an early age has, not only in a preschool environment, but also for the world.

What's the Risk of No Risk?

The boys in this photo were engaged in a serious experiment. They were working together to figure out how to get the gray tub to slide straight down the roof of the house without tumbling over and bouncing off. Some of the boys climbed up to the top of the roof to balance the tub on a wooden plank. They tied a string to the tub and threw the string down to the boy at the bottom, who is pictured in the midst of trying out the experiment.

If you were the adult on this playground and saw these four-, five-, and six-year-old boys at play, what would your initial response be? Would you:

a) stop them immediately because you think someone might get hurt?
b) remind them of the rules about no climbing on the playhouse roof?
c) ask them what interesting ideas they are up to and how you might help?
d) other.

In the child care program where I worked for 10 years, the staff had very different reactions to situations such as the one described here. A number of us were continually fearful that children would get hurt; others were concerned that if children didn't learn to follow rules, they would have a hard time following the rules when they got to public school. Some were worried about parent concerns and legal actions. Still others loved to join in and even help create the adventurous ideas and risky activities that children regularly pursued.

For a long time we didn't openly discuss our differences and there was an undercurrent of tension among us. Of course, because all of us wanted to keep the children safe, usually the most fearful teachers ended up persuading us that we should enforce the rules.

Things started to change when a new director was hired for our program. She immediately picked up on the divisions among the staff and was determined to have us air our differences and come together as a team. She wanted us to think through our ideas and define some shared agreements about what we thought was important. Just stopping children's risk-taking behavior and robotically following the rules were not options in her mind. She also advocated that children deserve and benefit from challenges and adventures that include risk. Their self-esteem grows, along with their physical and mental abilities as they negotiate risks appropriate for their personality and development. She wanted us to keep children safe, but insisted that it was just as important for us to guide them in becoming thoughtful decision-makers, able to one day assess and safely negotiate risky situations on their own. Her favorite saying was: "What risks do we take if we don't help children to negotiate risks?" She also truly believed that all of the teachers' perspectives were important to ensure children stay safe, as well as help them develop and thrive. She led staff meetings where we:

- discussed our life experiences and how they impact our reactions to these challenging situations with children.
- talked about the children's and families' points of view and what they deserve from us.
- reviewed the most current information from licensing and best practices for risk and safety in child care programs.

It was a long and sometimes bumpy process, but it really helped us come to respect each other's ideas. For example, in the situation above, we agreed that the children were capable of climbing the play house and negotiating the experiment, but the area wasn't designed as a fall zone so it wasn't a safe situation to let happen without adult supervision. We came to an agreement that for this particular situation, we would support the children's valuable collaboration and experimentation by making sure an adult was there to supervise the climbing to ensure that the area below was clear and safe. The children had a great celebration and new feelings of camaraderie within the group when the experiment was successful.

By studying situations in this way, our staff came to value the children's ideas and competence. We listened to each other and worked together to make sure activities were safe, while still encouraging rich learning opportunities for the children. The following outlines the elements that I've discovered help with this process.

Know Your Disposition Toward Risk

We all have different reactions to challenging situations and what we perceive as too risky. It is important for early childhood professionals to examine our views of these situations and make distinctions between our personal feelings and experiences, our coworkers' points of view, and children's strong desire for autonomy and competence. There isn't one right answer in these situations. Some of us may be too fearful and keep children from the opportunities they deserve and are capable of, while others encourage or allow risky situations that may not be safe for all children. It takes acknowledging our own disposition and working together with our colleagues to ensure children are safe, as well as appropriately challenged.

Ensure Your Own Comfort and Engagement

Teachers should be able to feel comfortable and engaged with what goes on in their work environment. Being asked to supervise activities that are outside our comfort zone isn't useful for us or the children. Also, having to stifle our excitement about offering new challenges for children creates a tense work environment. If we are feeling nervous or resentful about something that is going on, we should be able to acknowledge our disposition and need for support so our feelings don't negatively impact the children and each other. In the child care program described above, we successfully negotiated a situation like this to support everyone's comfort level and help children take appropriate risks for their skill and development.

Several of the older children in the program were eager and able to climb the smaller trees in our yard. A number of the teachers were very fearful of this and others really thought it was something that these children deserved to have as part of their childhood, just like they did when they were young. We decided that to keep the activity safe, the children needed supervision and guidance when they were climbing the trees. We agreed that the children had to be able to climb the tree on their own, a teacher needed to be right there to supervise, but no teachers could lift children up. Also, if children wanted to climb a tree they had to alert one of the "tree-climbing" teachers—those who were enthusiastic about supervising and able to support and keep the activity safe. If none of those teachers were available, then the children had to wait until they were. The children easily accommodated to these rules and came to respect all of the teachers' points of view.

Examine Your View of Children

Oftentimes we react from our own fears and stop children from negotiating a new challenge without taking into account their skills, competence, and determination. When I first began working with toddlers, I often stopped them from doing things I thought were too risky. Unconsciously, I saw them as fragile babies, not really aware or capable of negotiating the world around them or the situations they got themselves into. This photo of Shaelyn finding a way to reach the bar reflects one of the situations where I had this view. The playground was not designed for my 18-to-24-month-old group. Some of the equipment was too tall or too big for their smaller bodies and strength. This didn't stop the children. They regularly wanted to try out the equipment, finding ways to accommodate the challenges.

The strategy the children discovered for getting up to the bar was to move a chair underneath it, so they could climb up and suspend themselves above the ground. I immediately stopped the children from doing this and moved the chairs back to the table where they belonged. I noticed that I was stopping this chair-climbing many times a day, so one morning I decided to stay close to intervene if necessary, while observing and assessing Shaelyn as she negotiated this challenging task. It took her a great deal of effort to move the chair and careful coordination of her body to get up on top of the chair and avoid bumping her head on the bar. The hardest and most exhilarating part for her was holding on to the bar and lifting up her feet. It took all of her strength, as well as her courage. After a few seconds, she let herself drop back to the chair and grinned from ear to ear with her accomplishment. Studying her body language, I could see that she was quite capable of negotiating this challenge and the determination on her face told me she knew it!

The more I spend my days with these very young people the more I have changed my view of them. I have discovered that children usually pursue only the challenges that are within their abilities, using caution and remarkable problem-solving strategies. I have come to see that if I stay close to intervene if necessary, observe to get to know individual children's dispositions and skills, I can make sure I keep them safe while supporting their instinctive drive to challenge themselves and gain new competence. There is great reward in watching children's unwavering determination and seeing their elated faces when they accomplish something they have worked so hard on.

Inform Yourself and Practice Risk Management

There are numerous resources in the early childhood profession, as well as in the larger world to help us learn about risks and how to prevent serious accidents in our programs. Most of these resources make the distinction between a risk and a hazard. A risk is something that is possible to negotiate and may be appropriate for particular situations and children. A hazard is something that is inherently dangerous and needs to be remedied, such as a climbing structure with sharp edges or loose boards that could seriously injure children if they play on it.

There are also distinctions between risks and hazards that can result in serious injuries and even death, and those more common childhood accidents that cause bumps and bruises such as skinned knees, cuts, and scratches from prickly bushes. When these common accidents occur, children benefit from knowing that there are caring adults and other children to soothe their feelings and ease their pain with caring words and a colorful Band-Aid.® A useful resource for studying these distinctions is The Risk Pyramid in Margie Carter's and my book *Designs for Living and Learning*.[16]

Engage Families in Conversations about Challenge and Risk

Families have strong feelings and concerns about their children's safety, and rightly so. The director of our child care program believed in the importance of involving families in conversations and decisions along with the staff about everything, including the approaches we developed for challenge and risk. She held meetings where families worked with staff to study children's developmental tasks requiring challenge and risk. She formed a safety committee whose role was to help create policies and monitor the risk and safety issues in the program. Often staff and parent committees formed to help think through the benefits, risks, and rules for new programs, activities, or equipment that might involve unfamiliar challenges and potential risks for children, such as installing a new outdoor climber.

Create an Environment for Safe and Appropriate Challenges

The environment we provide for children is central to the work of offering children rich experiences while keeping them safe. We certainly must be vigilant about ensuring there are no hazards in order to prevent serious accidents. But we can also go too far in "childproofing" so that children have nothing interesting or challenging to do, making injuries more likely to occur. This was true in the first program I worked in with infants and toddlers. On behalf of keeping the children safe, the teachers had literally stripped the environment of almost everything except the furniture and a few toys.

An engaging environment for toddlers can prevent accidents.

I immediately began to add significantly more interesting materials in the environment for the children to use. At first the teachers were worried, but after a few weeks one of them said to me, "We used to have at least one accident report a day and now we rarely have any." Before, the only challenging activities in the environment for the children to do were to climb on the furniture or bump up against each other, so injuries occurred more often. Engaging the children's minds and bodies by enriching the environment helped focus their energy and instinctive appetite for exploration and interactions, which resulted in fewer falls and scuffles.

Remember, You are There

When our concern for safety leads programs to eliminate anything that might be a challenge for children, we diminish our role as teachers. I have heard this referred to as "teacher-proofing" the curriculum. It doesn't matter who the teacher is or what she does because there is a rule or prescribed way to do everything. I believe this leads to teachers taking a less active role in thinking through safety issues, as well as supporting children's learning.

I remind teachers that children are not alone in the room. We are there, too! It is our job to supervise children's safety, as well as provide for their curious minds and active bodies. When I show teachers the unusual activities and materials I offer children they often say to me, "Won't they break it?" "Won't they put it in their mouths?" "Won't they get hurt?" I always respond, "I'm right there doing this with them, so I won't let them get hurt." We should never offer children experiences that need

Toddlers earnestly learn to use scissors. They won't get hurt because the teacher is right there to supervise and coach them.

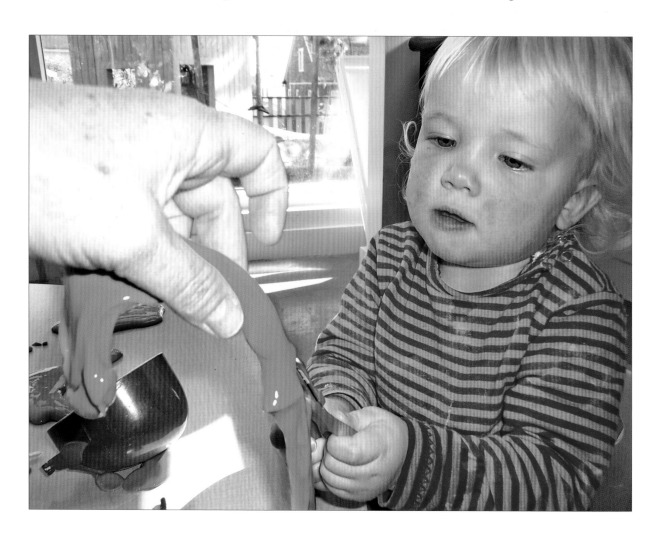

supervision if we aren't going to be there to support their safety, as well as their learning processes. We must take steps and be respected as competent professionals who are responsible for the safety, care, and education of the children we work with.

Provide Challenging Alternatives

Keeping children safe is paramount to the work we do every minute when we are with children. We must always stop or prevent situations that threaten children's well-being. But when we do intervene on behalf of children's safety, we can do it with the understanding that life has many challenges and risks, and children deserve experiences and tools to learn to negotiate on their own. The saying, "With few risks there are few rewards" is very true. Learning involves risk. Relationships involve risk. Feeling competent and confident in the world requires meeting a challenge and working to overcome it.

When children are involved in a situation we think is too risky or dangerous, rather than just stopping them, we can offer alternatives that keep them safe while preserving opportunities for them to develop to their fullest potential. This work requires that we pay attention to the children's perspectives, use our power thoughtfully, and act responsibly. We can ensure that children have a childhood where they feel exhilaration, while still being protected and supported by adults and their friends. We can support them in learning that determination pays off, and they can become competent decision-makers, able to assess risks, contribute to the well-being of others, and reap the rewards of their efforts.

SECTION 3
Seeing Children with Others

- Seeing Children's Eagerness for Relationships
- Helping Children to See Themselves and Each Other
- Seeing How Children See Us

Seeing children's competence and abilities, particularly when it comes to social skills and friendships, can provide powerful insights for teachers as they support the development of relationships among children and adults. The latest brain research suggests that children are keen social scientists able to see and understand the complex elements of being with others. Research findings show that children actually understand love and morality before they are three. The stories in this section suggest that seeing children's strengths in this area can enhance teacher's and children's feelings of joy and connection.

As you read the stories, consider taking up the following:

- *Study your own reactions to children's social interactions. Do you jump in to solve many problems? Do you notice conflict more often than when children are getting along?*
- *Do your own observations and documentation of how children see each other and how they see you. What insights do you gain and what new roles might you play to enhance the children's and your relationship?*

Seeing Children's Eagerness for Relationships

The photo "Rescuing Hug" had a huge impact on the way I see children's relationships with each other. This inspiring story describes the plight of premature twins struggling to live in separate incubators. When a nurse put them together, they began to thrive. The image of these fragile babies with arms wrapped around each other is astounding and celebrates the intuitive desire of human beings to reach out and support one another from the day we are born. Yet often the emphasis in our work with children is their inability to get along with each other. We learn as many skills and techniques as we can to manage children's behavior, focusing on their conflicts, continually reminding them of the rules, and regulating their behavior with time-out.

Imagine, instead, seeing children as already possessing the gifts for developing relationships and our role being to help them express this. I try to carry the image of the twins with me in my work to remind me of children's huge capacity for offering support and comfort, and accepting and benefiting from the gifts given by others. Rather than seeing their struggles with each other as negative, I have come to see that even children's challenging behaviors reveal that they are eager to connect and genuinely fascinated with one another's words, ideas, and actions.

I've come to the powerful realization that if I believe children have the capacity and desire for deep connections, then I support and coach them to live into their best selves. Transforming my view of children's challenging behaviors as they struggle to connect is no easy task, especially with the realities of negotiating daily life with large groups of young children. The following stories reflect the ongoing practice I use to see children's eagerness for relationships.

Notice and Marvel at Children's Positive Interactions with Each Other

I took this tender photo the first day that Oona transitioned from the toddler room into the two-year-old room. The questionable practice of moving children to a new room with new caregivers every year understandably left the usually confident Oona a bit tentative and fragile. I was stunned when Tommy intuitively knew what was needed. He joined Oona at the window, and I heard this conversation as they shared their two-year-old perspectives and began to cultivate a friendship.

> Tommy: *"I'm two and a half."*
> Oona: *"I'm two."*
> Tommy: *"You want to play at my house?" He tenderly put a hand on her shoulder.*
> Oona: *"My mommy says you can come to my house, too." They sat leaning close together at the window for a long while, silently watching children play in the yard.*

What a gift Tommy gave to Oona. His gentle physical gestures offered her reassurance and comfort during her first moments in this unfamiliar place. Tommy's words and the underlying meaning of them were immediately understood by Oona. He emboldened her with the shared power of being two-years-old, and his offer of friendship invited her into the security of each other's family life.

Because I make sure to notice moments like this over and over again in my work with even the youngest children, I have come to believe that all children have the capacity for empathy and kindness and are eager to play a role in helping others. I carry this belief with me as I support children to negotiate their conflicts as the following story suggests.

Coach Children to Offer Their Ideas and Competence

Taking care of babies was the most popular play theme among my group of one-year-olds. The children's play centered on imitating the caregiving tasks they experienced—rocking babies, putting the bottles into the dolls' mouths, and pushing them in the stroller. One morning during playtime, T'Kai was playing with some babies, when Wynsome came over and grabbed one of his dolls. He complained loudly as she ran away and sat in the rocking chair with the doll.

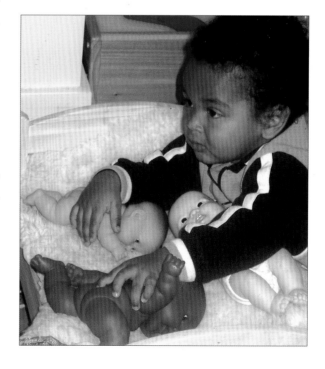

Earlier in the week I had noticed that Wynsome had discovered the colorful crocheted squares and was using them to carefully cover the babies to create a cozy bed. Rather than focusing on Wynsome's disruptive behavior of taking the doll away from T'Kai, I decided to offer her a way to show her competence. I suggested that Wynsome show T'Kai her idea of making a bed for the babies and she immediately took up my offer. She eagerly gave T'Kai a doll and some blankets and a bottle, and showed him how to make a bed for the baby. T'Kai was a bit surprised that Wynsome gave him the doll because he was so used to defending his territory. He happily accepted her coaching, making his own bed for the baby.

Later, when I studied the photos I took of Wynsome during this baby play, I was stunned by the realization of the power I have over how children come to see themselves and their abilities in the world. If I focus on Wynsome's struggle to connect, it can lead to feelings of shame where she feels and acts like a "bad girl." Instead, I want to offer Wynsome and other children the opportunity to make a contribution which, in turn, builds their confidence and sense of belonging. This was a powerful moment for Wynsome because she was able to see the possibilities for herself as a competent, caring person.

Use Documentation to Show Children Their Positive Social Interactions

I noticed that the bed-making play that Wynsome demonstrated immediately expanded the children's script for baby play. I began to make books with detailed photos of children's ideas and activities throughout the classroom. Studying these books had an impact on the children's play, as they tried out what they saw each other doing in the books, working cooperatively, and with more complexity.

If this was true for expanding the children's play, I reasoned that specifically showing them their positive social interactions could grow their abilities to connect. I decided to make homemade books with detailed photos of children's positive interactions so they could see their own and each other's ideas and competencies.

I was inspired by one of the children's favorite books called *I Can Share!*

by Karen Katz.[17] Each page depicts a particular social struggle, such as: "That's my bike, you can't ride on my bike." Followed by a page that says: "But maybe you can get on the back and I'll take you for a ride." The children became enthralled, wide-eyed, and attentive whenever I read this book. This led me to the idea of documenting their struggles and successes with relationships and making a book using this same format.

The children loved the book I made about them, even more than the original version, and wanted me to read it over and over. The words and photos in our book acknowledged the powerful and conflicting feelings the children had in these moments of relating to each other. Studying these books together reinforced what the children already knew about working together and reminded them how to use these positive behaviors with each other more.

I continue the practice of always looking for children's positive social behaviors to document and make visible to them and to me. I observe children working together throughout the room and document their activities through note taking and asking myself these questions:

- What specific things do children do and say that indicate they are connecting with each other and building relationships?
- How do they use objects or materials in their play to communicate their ideas?
- What challenges or conflicts occur?
- What do children do and say to resolve their differences?

I make these observation notes and photos into homemade books with titles such as "We know how to work together." I include specific photos and details of what the children say and do that reflects what they know about working together. I regularly read these books with the children, inviting them to add more ideas over time.

What I've come to understand is that the most important work I do to see a child in positive ways is within me. I must continually work to transform my own view of children's behaviors, see their points of view, and strive to uncover how what I am seeing reveals the children's deep desire, eagerness, and capacity for relationships. There is no more important or rewarding work than this.

Helping Children to See Themselves and Each Other

Seeing children—noticing the details of their actions and words and seeking their perspective to catch a glimpse of how they experience the world—brings joy and deeper understanding to my work and life. Over the years I've cultivated the practice of slowing down and observing closely to see the child's point of view. I've discovered that when I intentionally share the details of what I notice with children, many positive things unfold.

Young children at play are deeply engaged in the here-and-now of what they are doing. They immerse themselves in the wonders around them, noticing the world in a very different way than adults do. While adults can bring meta-cognition to an experience, children don't regularly think about their thinking as they work. More often, their focus shifts and unfolds based on sensory explorations and discoveries that are a result of actions and reactions.

When I offer children descriptions of the remarkable things I see them doing and what I think they may be noticing or thinking about, they engage more deeply, repeating their actions and adding new ideas to their work. They regularly respond to my offerings by showing and telling me about their discoveries. I've noticed that children who build on the details are motivated to add more, and they stick with an activity for longer periods of time. Revisiting their ideas seems to help children organize their thoughts and actions and use the information to plan for and extend their investigations and learning.

Strategies for Helping Children See Themselves

As I gather detailed observations, I think about and write directly to the child I'm observing, as in the following story of Charlie. I use a rich vocabulary and suggest what I think might be the child's idea. I take photos of what I see, focusing on the children in relationship to materials and each other. Collecting information in these ways allows me to study their perspectives more effectively and provides me with tools to offer children back their work and ideas in a variety of ways.

The table was filled with hundreds of buttons that invited children to immerse themselves in the treasure of exploration and discovery. Charlie, you immediately leaned over the tray of buttons and thoughtfully picked up and studied one button at a time. I wondered what you noticed as you carefully examined each button. You showed remarkable attention to detail as you worked, methodically sorting and classifying the buttons into piles and then creating a design with the buttons based on the attributes you noticed. Though I didn't hear you speak, I was fascinated by the intensity in your eyes, your facial expressions, and your body language as you worked.

Interacting with Children

Inspired by my colleague Tom Drummond's writing, *Enterprise Talk*, I avoid giving directions or asking questions, and instead offer information and descriptions about what I see.[18] There is a shift in my role and I pay closer attention to what comes out of my mouth. As a result, I notice more details and really begin to see children and the complexity of their work. I use words and gestures to reveal to children what I see. I ask the children if I can try out what they are doing and describe my experiences as I work. I also take photos and show children images of what they have done. Through this work together, children build their capacity to initiate and regulate their own ideas and actions.

I approached my work with Charlie this way: describing the details I noticed in his body language and the work he was doing with the buttons. As a result, Charlie eagerly shared his thinking with me about what he was discovering, pointing to the buttons and naming their similarities and differences. He leaned in to study the photos on my camera of him engaged in the work.

Helping Children See Each Other

In addition to helping children see their own work, I also help them notice each other's work and ideas. I describe the details of what I observe one child doing to another child and suggest we watch closely to learn more. I notice that the simple act of helping children see each other launches them into descriptions and deeper discussions about what's on their minds. The children learn from each other and try out the ideas they see and hear. This enhances their skills and the repertoire of possibilities that the children bring to the investigation, which in turn, expands their collaboration and the amount of time they spend on an activity. This is exactly what happened with Charlie and a child working next to him. As I invited her to notice what he was doing, she eagerly joined in, working with him to search for specific buttons to add to the design.

Representations of Children's Ideas in the Environment

Recognizing how powerful my words and actions are in sharing children's work with them, I have begun to leave concrete representations of their work in the environment:

- I make photo displays using detailed photos of their work to put on a wall or shelf near the materials the children are using.
- I create homemade books with photos and descriptions for children to revisit their own ideas and the ideas of other children in the classroom.
- I make charts with the steps we discovered about how to do something.

Revisiting the details of the many actions and ideas that unfold throughout our days helps children bring more focus and intention to their work, and enables them to begin from a more complex point in their investigations.

Creating a Classroom Culture

Really seeing children and helping children see themselves has become the foundation of my work with both older and younger children. We have an environment filled with many possibilities for rich investigation and learning.

As we engage in the environment, the children and I intentionally notice the details of our actions, perspectives, and discoveries and make these visible to each other with words, gestures, and images. Observing closely for the often surprising and complex details of the children's actions and interactions enhances all of our days. Staying present in the moment with children and helping them see the remarkable ways they immerse themselves in learning about the world has become our classroom culture. Living and learning together with children in this way is so very rich and rewarding for us all!

In the button play, Melissa figured out she could form the letters of her name with the buttons. She gathered up all of the construction paper pieces to use as the background for each of the letters of her name. Another child began to complain, saying Melissa was taking all the paper. I described the interesting details of what Melissa was doing and encouraged Melissa to tell her classmate her idea about using the paper and the buttons. The other child

became intrigued with the idea and the two of them worked together to make letters on each piece of paper. Because the girls communicated and shared the details, it helped them work together and encouraged them to see that sharing ideas is more valuable than only negotiating the use of "stuff."

Anthony was working with a paintbrush and watercolor. I sat next to him, watching for a while. I didn't want to intrude on his focus so I waited until I observed a pattern in what he was doing, indicating to me that he had possibly made a discovery that he was repeating. I noticed he was using the brush very carefully to make small marks of paint, so I described in detail what I saw and pointed to the marks and the brush. He immediately examined the brush and studied it as he made the marks again. He continued doing this same

action over and over again covering the page with the paint marks. Lily, sitting next to him, was listening and watching what Anthony and I did together. She brought the jar of blue watercolor closer and tried Anthony's technique. He protested (with a toddler squeal) when Lily took the jar. I suggested, "Look, Anthony. Lily liked your idea and wants to try it. She's making small marks of paint on her paper just like you did and she needs the blue paint to do it." He watched her actions closely. Toddlers show a great deal of interest in each other, and Anthony demonstrated this when he was helped to see how Lily shared his perspective. They began to move the jar back and forth between them, continuing to make the marks and watching as they worked.

Seeing How Children See Us

By Deb Curtis and Lorrie Baird

It was a beautiful fall day and the playground was alive with the activity of children and teachers engaged in play. A teacher was watching the children in the sand box when Charlie approached her and asked a simple question: "Are you happy?" The teacher, curious and a bit surprised by the question, replied; "Yes, of course I am." Charlie responded with all the wisdom of a four-year-old: "Then you should tell your face that!"

Charlie reminds us in this startling moment that children have laser-like attention for everything we do and say. They are skillful social scientists, learning about themselves, relationships, and the world by carefully observing the people around them. In fact, children are primed to see us. Infants are born with the ability to see best at a distance of 8 to 14 inches, the perfect distance for gazing up from the arms of their mothers, fathers, and caregivers, the perfect distance to begin to build connections and relationships and learn from seeing us.

As people who are fascinated with how children see the world, we have been reflecting together about the notion of how children see us:

- Do our faces show delight or consternation?
- Do our hands soothe or scold?
- Do our voices invite singing together or command silence?
- Do our bodies overwhelm children with our size and power or wrap them up in comfort?

As keen observers, children notice the smallest details of our body language, tone of voice, and movements. Our interactions and presence have a powerful impact on how children view themselves and us. With this power comes an opportunity, as well as tremendous responsibility, for us to use it well. So, how can we study the details of what children see in us and what these details may communicate? It begins with being conscientious about how we want children to see us and taking the time to examine ourselves.

Study Yourself

To study yourself is among the most important professional development tasks you can take up. How you physically and verbally respond to children and how they see you grows from your beliefs and values, your view of children, and the role you hope to play in their lives. This makes it essential to spend time developing and revisiting core values for your work:

- To begin, brainstorm a list of what you believe children deserve when they spend their days with you.
- Next, generate a specific list of the roles you will play to support these core values.
- Share your ideas with others to help them become deeply planted in your mind.
- As you interact with children, be attentive to your actions and how you communicate the values you hope to encourage in them.

Notice Your Body

Research on body language suggests that we can't ignore the fact that our bodies, and the way we physically present ourselves to children, communicates more than the actual words we speak. Our size and how we position our bodies, the closeness or distance to children, how slow or fast we move, all have an impact on the much smaller people we spend our days with. When you are with children, be mindful of your body:

- Are you towering over the children or down at their level?
- Is your body tense or relaxed?
- How fast are you moving?
- How are the children experiencing and responding to your physical presence?

Celebrate Your Hands

When you think about your hands and all the ways you use them each day in your work, it's mind boggling! How often do you hold a child's hand, wipe away a tear or runny nose, mix paint and play-dough, clap along with a tune or for a child's accomplishments, demonstrate how to cut with scissors, calm with a back rub at nap time, write a note or type an observation, or wash your hands for the millionth time? Children notice the intimate details of our hands at work and so should we.

- Take note and take care of your hands.

- Frame a collage of close-up photos of your hands to put on the wall to remind you of their importance.
- Share hand massages with the children and your coworkers using special soap and lots of soothing lotions. Celebrate your hands together!

Make Friends with Your Face

As the saying goes, "Your eyes are a window to your soul"—as are your facial expressions the windows for children to see you and in turn, see themselves and the world. Children pick up the smallest nuances, like a twinkle in your eye or a grimace around your mouth, and come to understand how to "read" people and complex emotions. Stop to consider the powerful impact facial expressions have on your interpretation of an interaction. You have been reading faces and developing your own facial expressions since you were born and do it now instantaneously and unconsciously. You can work to be more conscious of what your face and eyes communicate by studying them.

- Start by recalling situations you may have had with children during the day.
- As you remember, let yourself respond with your face and eyes as you look in a mirror:
  - What does your face communicate?
  - How might children see and understand what your eyes are saying?
- Have someone videotape you in your work with children.
- Study your facial expressions, as well as your body language and tone of voice.
- Notice what the children's points of view might be to your presence and actions:
  - Are children seeing you how you would like them to see you?

Children See When You See Them

One of the most powerful ways to impact how children see you is to carefully observe them and find ways to let them know you see *them*. The following ordinary moment shows the power of a teacher's conscious actions to see and be seen with three-year-old Austin.

"You want them all"

Austin's teacher is observing him working carefully to fill the metal container to the very top with a variety of wooden balls and rings. He spends a great deal of time opening and closing the transparent lid, each time looking inside when it's open, and looking again through the lid when it's closed. He dumps it out and fills it again. Another child approaches and tries to take some of the balls as Austin protests loudly, scurrying to round up the balls to fill the container. Both children grab the container and pull at it. Austin holds on tighter and wins the tug of war.

His teacher calmly says, "Austin, you have been working on a careful idea of filling that container and you need all of the balls. Kai, you had a different idea, but Austin wasn't done." She says nothing else about the conflict, sharing, or taking turns, and Kai easily moves on to another activity.

Austin now walks around happily holding the container, while at the same time protecting the materials from other children.

His teacher smiles at him and says, "You are enjoying having all of those, Austin." He trustingly brings the container over to the teacher and eagerly shows her what's inside.

She says with a smile, "It's filled to the very top! Thanks for sharing with me."

Austin smiles broadly, sits down next to the teacher, and begins to dump and fill the container again.

When it's time to clean up, Austin's teacher, with a compassionate look on her face tells him, "It's going to be really sad for me to ask you to put those toys away, because you have been working so carefully with them all morning." Austin moves away, clutching the container tightly, while the teacher and the other children clean up. After a few minutes of walking around and watching the cleanup, Austin comes back to the teacher and with a smile, hands over the container. When it's time to go, Austin looks up at his teacher with a smile, takes her hand, and walks to the lunchroom.

This simple story of Austin and his teacher illustrates that children know when their teachers are truly present with them. They see when our words and bodies communicate that we are listening with our hearts and minds. When we engage with children in this deeply respectful way, observing them closely, while being continually aware of ourselves, children will come to see us as we hope to be seen, and in turn, we will see children as they deserve to be seen and known.

Seeing Children and Theories of Development

- Seeing Children Find Endless Possibilities
- Seeing and Supporting Children's Kinship with the Natural World
- Seeing Children Fully Immersed in Sensory Exploration
- Seeing and Appreciating Children's Humor
- Seeing Children's Pleasure with Food
- Can Babies Read and Write?

When you see yourself as a teacher–researcher in your daily practice with children you can enhance the intellectual, emotional, and even spiritual aspects of your work. With every detailed observation, there are a multitude of theories and research findings that you can use to make meaning of what you are seeing. As you study these aspects of teaching and learning, the depth of your knowledge and the repertoire of possibilities you have for working with children grows. The stories in this section offer a variety of innovative lenses with which to see children.

As you read the stories, consider the following:

- *Which of the articles do you find most fascinating? Why?*
- *What new insights do you have as a result of reading about the variety of ways to make meaning of your work with children?*
- *What areas of development or research are you curious about that you would like to study in your work with children?*

Seeing Children Find Endless Possibilities

By Deb Curtis and The United Way Bright Beginnings Toddler Teacher Cohort

We have been observing toddlers for several years now, and each time, we are more astonished with the brilliance we see in these very young people. We gather together quarterly in each other's classrooms, offer children interesting materials to explore, then we observe and document what unfolds as they play. After the observation, we meet for several hours to study our notes and photos, and think together about the significance of what we have seen for the children's learning and our own.

We feared that the ice balls with objects frozen inside that we offered recently would have limited potential for engaging the children for very long. We wondered aloud what the children would do after the ice melted and there were only a few objects left to play with. The children quickly showed us that we were greatly mistaken in our assessment of their capacity to see possibilities. The investigations and discoveries that unfolded over the next hour were beyond anything we could have predicted.

So Many Possibilities

The ice balls were large and heavy so they attracted the children immediately. The children were drawn to the challenge of lifting and carrying them around the space and transporting them back and forth between the containers. The ice was cold to touch and taste, and the children lingered while licking and chewing on it for quite a while.

One of the children discovered that when he dropped the ice balls they broke open, shattering into smaller pieces. The many different sized ice pieces now became the center of attention. Some children filled up the containers with them and still others kept throwing the pieces to the ground, eager to see them break into even tinier bits. The children worked diligently to find every piece, large and small, to toss to the ground, watching the exhilarating transformation.

The ice was transforming in another way: melting from a solid to a liquid and puddles were forming all over the mat. The puddles became an action-packed new adventure. The children sat in the puddles, slapped the water with their hands, and ran through the puddles, splashing up and down in them, causing water to fly through the air.

Even after all the ice melted and the puddles dispersed, the children still weren't done. The red buckets captured their attention and they began to use them in many ways. Some children happily put them on their heads, laughing together about this comic discovery. Others found a way to sit inside the buckets, manipulating their arms and bodies to get them to spin around and around like an amusement park ride.

Last, but not least, the buckets became a launching pad for energetic jumping. Children with different comfort and skill levels took up this activity. Some were able to launch themselves high and far. One child felt challenged, yet proud, and successful as she gingerly stepped off the bucket. The children made a collaborative, thrilling game of it, taking turns jumping together, over and over again.

Optimal Experiences

Needless to say, we left this play session filled with pleasure and awe with what we had witnessed. Along with the stunning number of possibilities for exploration the children came up with, the mood of their play was just as striking. There was constant change, but it was not frenetic. The children were intensely focused, yet peaceful, with an easy flow to their activities. One child would start an idea and others would take it up. Then another idea would spring up and that would spread with ease and delight throughout

the group. The growing of ideas unfolded continuously throughout the playtime. The children recognized their camaraderie, satisfied with their ability to see and share each other's ideas.

This experience reflects the concept of "flow" as described by psychologist Mihaly Csikszentmihalyi.[19] His famous investigations of "optimal experience" have revealed that what makes an experience genuinely satisfying is a state of consciousness called "flow." During flow, people typically experience deep enjoyment, a sense of timelessness, focused creativity, and total immersion with learning and life. We have come to believe that when toddlers are given time together, enough space, and open-ended materials, "flow" comes naturally to them.

The Role of Adults

As we observed the children, we were quickly drawn in to their mood and interests. While we supervised for safety, we mostly let things happen. It never seemed necessary to jump in to stop anything. Instead we marveled at the children's abilities and the way they approached their explorations like scientists. Their shared pleasure and interests charmed us. We found ourselves smiling and laughing at the surprising endeavors they took up. Perhaps we joined the children in a state of "flow" by merely watching them.

Seeing Brain Development and Learning Theory

The children's work revealed the brain development and learning theories we have been studying. We saw strong evidence of the flexibility of the children's brains as they pursued never-ending possibilities for exploring and learning with the materials. The children were powerful learning machines as Alison Gopnik describes them.[20] They used the best skills and dispositions of scientists as they initiated and tried out their theories, noticed cause-and-effect, and built from one discovery to another.

We also saw Piaget's schema theory magnified. The children's play showed repeated patterns, which represent threads of thought that they are pursuing to learn about the world. The descriptions of schemas matched the children's actions. We saw:

- *Transformation:* The children engaged with watching and making changes to the ice and water.
- *Trajectory:* The children were engrossed with throwing ice, spinning in tubs, and jumping off of buckets again and again.
- *Transporting:* The children enjoyed moving ice from one container to another, and carrying the large balls all around the room.
- *Enveloping and Enclosing:* The children used buckets to fit over their heads and to skillfully get themselves all the way into the buckets to sit and spin.[21]

Reflections on Our Own Learning

The nature of our work with toddlers keeps us busy. We spend our days keeping children moving, eating and sleeping, changing diapers, wiping noses, planning activities, and keeping the peace. Slowing down to notice and marvel at the details of the children's ideas and abilities is not an easy task. Our work as a group has helped us realize the importance of pausing to see the children's ideas because we always see rich experiences grow.

- We have come to know that children have many ideas and often really don't need ours.
- We understand that we can keep children safe while giving them more opportunities to be challenged and joyful.
- We are in awe when we take time to see the amazing brilliance of children. We never want to lose sight of the natural wonder and innate drive young children have to explore and learn deeply.

We are also inspired to see the power of reflective practice and thinking together as a group for our own learning and the affirmation of the bigger meaning of our work with young children.

Seeing and Supporting Children's Kinship with the Natural World

If a child is to keep alive his inborn sense of wonder without any such gift from the fairies, he needs the companionship of at least one adult who can share it, rediscovering with him the joy, excitement, and mystery of the world we live in.

~Rachel Carson

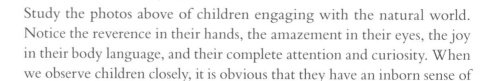

Study the photos above of children engaging with the natural world. Notice the reverence in their hands, the amazement in their eyes, the joy in their body language, and their complete attention and curiosity. When we observe children closely, it is obvious that they have an inborn sense of wonder and affinity for nature, which enriches their lives and ours.

Yet children are spending less and less time outdoors so they are losing their enchantment with the natural world, and even worse, they come to fear it. Information has become available regarding the alarming consequences to children's physical, cognitive, emotional, and spiritual health and well-being when they don't play outside. Needless to say, our environment will continue to suffer if children grow into adults who don't have experiences where they learn to love and protect the planet.

In response, there are many local, national, and international initiatives designed to promote nature education and keep children connected to the natural world, including the Nature Action Collaborative for Children through the World Forum Foundation (www.worldforumfoundation.org/nature) and the Dimensions Educational Research Foundation and Arbor Day Foundation's collaborative program, Nature Explore (www.natureexplore.org). These resources help us remember the vital importance of protecting children's kinship with nature.

Offering Children Experiences with Nature is Difficult

It's true that many child care centers are lacking in natural environments. The emphasis in programs is more often about rules and regulations for children's health and safety, and concerns about allergies, the weather, and getting dirty.

It's also difficult for us to take groups of children into natural environments with inadequate ratios of adults to children. There are even more challenges to providing experiences in nature when we work with groups of infants and toddlers. Add to that adults who are disconnected from the natural world because they spend very little time outdoors, and those who have fear and anxiety being in nature. It's no wonder we stay indoors most of the time.

Cultivating Our Own Connections to Nature

In order to move beyond the barriers, fears, and inconveniences, it is crucial that we find ways to cultivate our own deep connections to the natural world. We can learn about the importance of being outdoors from books, seminars, and the Internet, but the best teachers we have are the children we spend our days with as they embrace the natural world around them.

Searching for the Natural World

I shared a remarkable experience in nature with a group of toddlers and their teachers from the United Way Bright Beginnings Quality Improvement Program in Houston, Texas. For a number of years I have been working with small groups of teachers to study approaches to teaching and learning. Our recent focus was on supporting children's connections to the natural world. Our plan was to provide children with experiences in nature and then observe and study their responses and the role we could play to strengthen their connections to the natural world.

I was concerned about how much nature we would find surrounded by the glass, steel, and concrete buildings of the city, and in the manicured office parks and schools where these programs are located. But it was important to use the environments in the child care centers where the teachers worked so experiences with nature would be easily accessible. My hope was that teachers would rediscover and fall in love with nature right outside their doors, so they would be motivated to share these experiences with their children.

Reawakening Our Connections

We started our work by scouting the yard to find natural materials for the children to explore. Our ongoing study of children over the years helped us have a good idea of what they would be drawn to: items with texture, color, and movement, and loose parts to investigate and transform. And, of course, we made sure everything on the playground was non-toxic.

From what initially looked like a place lacking in natural wonder and beauty, we discovered that the simple splendor of nature surrounds us if we just stop to take notice. As they searched the yard, the teachers called out to each other "Oh," and "Ah," eagerly sharing their excitement about the insects they found, the complex structures of leaves, and the intricate details of an open flower they could see through magnifying glasses.

We spread a blanket on the ground, brought out some trays and baskets, and used the materials we collected to create a beautiful Invitation to share with the children. We were astonished at the transformation we made to the yard. Right outside the door of this typical child care setting, nature was waiting for us with grass, rocks, leaves, pods, and small creatures to attract and hold the children's and our attention for hours, days, even a lifetime.

Learning from Children

Toddlers often have a reputation for a lack of self-control and short attention span, so we were surprised when the children didn't dive right in to play with the materials. Instead, they approached the Invitation gradually with looks of awe, wonder, and respect in their eyes. When the children began to engage with the materials, they observed closely, touched, rubbed, and squeezed to study all aspects of the objects. They quickly learned to use the magnifying glasses to enhance their view. The toddlers worked with a quiet focus and purpose. Several times the children put the berries and

leaves up to their noses to smell them. Again, we were surprised because none of the children put anything in their mouths. Their attention was focused on the many other interesting things they could do with the objects.

The children's close study led to a variety of explorations and new discoveries, including making sounds by shaking leaves, tapping rocks together, and dropping pods on trays and into wooden bowls. Each of their investigations inspired further investigation: dropping objects into bowls evolved into careful sorting and arranging of berries and plums into the bowls and baskets. A few of the children seemed to be noticing and classifying by size as they placed the berries in containers.

As toddlers often do, their attention turned to exuberant ways to make the natural objects move. This developed into a group effort as the children invented a game together to roll and bounce the green berries on large black trays. We were delighted as we watched them laugh uproariously, shaking the tray until all of the berries flew off, and then enthusiastically filling the tray and starting the game again.

We also observed the children gently studying insects, intently watching their movement as they crawled around on the ground and on the children's hands. The children were eager to have a relationship with these fragile, living creatures. We marveled at the affinity and care for living things they brought to their investigations.

After more than an hour, we reluctantly interrupted the children's exploration for lunch. During our time together, the children:

- helped us see nature's patterns, textures, rhythms, and all the possibilities for engaging our hearts and minds.
- showed us the roots of scientific inquiry.
- taught us how to use our senses to examine and make discoveries, to try out ideas, notice cause-and-effect, and the impact our actions have on the world around us.
- gave us the gift of seeing the joy, mystery, and excitement in the simple beauty of nature.
- reawakened our own sense of wonder and appreciation for our kinship with the remarkable natural world surrounding us.

Studying and Celebrating Our Experiences

We spent a full day reflecting on our experiences with the children in the natural world by:

- studying photos and video clips and analyzing the children's ideas and interactions.
- spending more time outdoors near the office building where we held our meeting.
- gathering treasures from the natural world.
- creating stunning displays of natural materials.
- gaining inspiration from their observations of the children to study and enjoy what they found.
- writing letters of appreciation to Mother Nature to reinforce their new connections.

Letters of Appreciation to Mother Nature

Dear Purple Flower,

You were beautiful when I laid my eyes on you peeking through the fence, swaying in the wind. When I pulled you off the branch, you were so full of life. I put you in a paper bag and brought you inside to show my toddler teacher friends. When I took you out of the bag, you looked lifeless. Your beautiful petals started to close up and got a little wrinkled. So now when I look at you, I wish I wouldn't have picked you off the branch. I should just admire you every time I see you when I pass by.

—Lorna Patterson

As I walk through the path of beauty the smell and look of the beautiful, bright pink flowers catch my eye. The texture of the green leaf calls me over. I accept the invitation. I introduce myself by feeling the pattern of the leaf. I am amazed. I notice the beautiful color of leaves. "Purplish color," I say as I begin to count them one by one. Finally I reach the end and I'm done. I notice a dead bunch of leaves. This lets me know that winter's near.

—Daun Jones

Letter to Zion

Experiences with children in nature can reawaken our own connections with the natural world and move us to share these joyful experiences. An inspiring example of this comes from Shannon McClellan, a consultant with the Bright Beginnings program. She has become committed to sharing the natural world with the children of Bright Beginnings, as well as with her own grandchildren. After a recent trip to the beach, she wrote this lovely letter to her one-year-old grandson Zion as a keepsake for her time with him.

Shannon's loving words and experience with her grandson show us the elegant simplicity and powerful impact sharing nature with children can bring. You, too, can follow Shannon and Zion's tiny footsteps and become a companion for children in the natural world.

Dear Zion,

Today was your very first visit to the beach in Galveston, Texas. You were very excited when I put you down to experience the soft sand. You wandered off from time to time as if you already knew your way around. You noticed your shadow as you took one step at a time. You looked down as your feet began to sink into the soft, gray sand. As I watched, I wondered what you were feeling as you took those tiny steps. You never took your eyes off the water. What were you thinking as you saw the waves coming toward you with such force?

Zion, what a brave person you are. You walked around without any fear of an environment you have never seen. Watching you enlightened me to how important it was for you to have this experience. It made me feel wonderful knowing I gave you this opportunity. My heart was filled with joy knowing that you are a person who is curious and imaginative and able to explore as a scientist. You helped me realize that nature is an expression of reality that can touch me in a sensitive and passionate way.

Seeing Children Fully Immersed in Sensory Exploration

By Jess Guiney, Sheena Wilton, and Deb Curtis

Jessica and Isabella were immediately drawn to the new chalk available on the patio. As soon as they saw the big basket, they found an open space and began testing the colors. They seemed attracted to the brighter shades, choosing to use them first. They began experimenting with differing amounts of pressure as they filled in the space with chalk. Isabella worked slowly, noticing the brightness of her colors. Jessica worked quickly, examining the amount of chalk dust that was accumulating as she moved her chalk across the ground like a windshield wiper.

When Jessica pointed out how much colorful dust had gathered around them, Isabella was intrigued to slowly and quietly explore it. First, she moved a little pile around with one finger. Then, she swished her entire hand back and forth over the dust, mixing the colors together. Finally, Isabella blew the chalk dust across the cement, moving it in yet another way. After most of her work was beautifully blurred, she looked up and said, "It looks like a wish."

As the girls continued to fill the space around them with different shades of chalk, they noticed more about how the colors blended and spread.

As they spread the dust with their hands:
"Look at how much pink there is now!"
"The blue is so big now!"

As they mixed the dust:
"We can make a new color."
"Yeah, a new kind of pink!"

Jessica also looked at Isabella and saw that her black pants were covered in the chalk she was sitting in, "Your pants are now that blue!" Smiling, Isabella stood up to examine herself, then made a deliberate choice to sit in the red chalk dust. Happy with the way her pants looked, she filled the ground with the two colors and stretched her legs on top of them!

After Jessica moved on, Isabella stayed engaged with the chalk, continuing to watch the amount of chalk dust grow, and mixing it with her hands. Using different colors and creating little piles, Isabella waited to gather a certain amount before blending them together. "I'm making a wish," she shared, "'cause it just looks like it!"

Later, Jessica and Isabella returned to the chalk, and began to fill in a large portion of the patio with the same vibrant colors that had been so attractive to them earlier. The two used the chalk in a variety of ways, rubbing it on its side, holding it upright and making lines, and using their hands to spread the dust around. As they worked, the girls discussed their drawing:

"It's an ocean. We're drawing the whole ocean!"
"And there are so many colors in the ocean that we're putting pink and blue!"
"And you can see, here, the waves," Jessica said, as she moved her hands through the chalk dust representing the movement of the ocean.

Jessica studied the chalk she was using. "Look," she observed. "They're shrinking! They're getting smaller and smaller!" "Yeah," Isabella agreed, looking at the chalk. "And this one is the biggest 'cause I didn't really use it yet.

And the blue one is the smallest 'cause we used it for the whole, whole ocean!" The girls continued to make comparisons about the qualities of the chalk:

> *"This one is smoothest."*
> *"This one is pointier than the others."*
> *"This one has the most dust!"*

Soon, they were deliberately changing the shape and texture of the chalk by rubbing it against the rough concrete.

> *"This one is shrinking again! It's smaller and smaller!"*
> *"Now I can make this one have a point!"*

As Jessica looked closely at the chalk, she acknowledged the color of her hands—pink with chalk dust—for the first time. "Look at my pink,

pink hands. They're pink from the ocean, and a little blue." She then made note of the chalk dust on Isabella's face. "It's like make-up! We're putting on make-up!"

Jessica spread the chalk dust from her hands onto her cheeks, and used a finger to gather some blue dust from the ground for her nose. "Look," she and Isabella called together. "Look at us! Will you take pictures to send to our moms?"

A Drawing Experience or a Sensory Experience?

We recently brought this story to our planning time to share the photos and notes we had collected of Jessica and Isabella working with the chalk. As we discussed what unfolded, we became more and more fascinated with the chalk work of the children. We were particularly struck by how the girls immersed themselves in the chalk, covering their faces, hands, arms, and bodies. Was this a sensory experience rather than the drawing experience we had planned? Our conversations greatly expanded our ideas about the nature of sensory exploration for young children.

Before these conversations, we thought of sensory experiences in typical ways: water play, play-dough, sand play, and finger-paint, where children mix, spill, splash, and make a mess. We didn't consider chalk a sensory activity. But observing Jessica and Isabella's immersion in the chalk helped us go beyond the usual way of seeing. We expanded our idea of sensory experiences to study the notion of aesthetic experiences.

Webster's definition of "aesthetics" is an abstract concept meaning "perception" in Greek. Aesthetics offer a focused and metaphorical way of knowing and experiencing the world that involves engaging with your senses, feelings, attitudes, processes, and responses to objects and experiences. Aesthetic experiences involve awareness and appreciation of the beauty found in the world and allow us to become totally lost in the moment. This definition certainly described the girls' experiences with the chalk.

Space and Materials as an Aesthetic Experience

As Isabella and Jessica explored the chalk, their experience was informed by the space in which they worked. The chalk was carefully presented in a large basket with a handle. As the girls worked, they scattered the many pieces of chalk around themselves, making all of their options visible, and each color easy to reach.

The patio is large and boasts a sizable patch of pavement that is free of traffic. Additionally, there are many variations in the texture of the pavement, some spots being rougher than others. As the girls explored, the fact that the surface they were drawing on was large and that it changed subtly, seemed to enhance their experience.

The quality of the chalk also added to the girls' explorations. The intensity of the colors and the large amount of dust that the chalk produced contributed to the girls' deep focus on the materials and to the long period of time that they were engaged.

We noticed the girls experimenting with each piece of available chalk and ultimately settling on those that were the brightest. Later, we were struck by the girls' almost exclusive use of "hot pink" and "bright blue." We noted that the girls were using chalk marks with great variation in line quality, and filling big, solid patches of pavement. They used full body movements to make the chalk marks, move the dust around the space, and apply pressure to change the chalk from solid to dust. They delighted in covering themselves with the colorful dust. The girls showed us that chalk offers much more than a drawing experience. As they immersed themselves in the chalk, we learned that chalk also provides a rich sensory experience.

Uncovering Emotion and Metaphor

The marked change in Jessica and Isabella's intention during the course of their work with the chalk intrigued us. Initially, the girls were eager to explore the chalk to discover its many possibilities by getting to know it as intimately as possible, physically and emotionally. At this time, they didn't seem to have a sense of ownership of the space where they worked, and instead, appeared entirely focused on being with the chalk. We observed that the girls used the chalk deliberately, drawing a vast ocean, comparing the dust to "wishes" and sharing their discovery of the chalk as "make-up." They understood each other in a deep way, fully sharing the emotional and physical experience of the chalk with each other. These joyful connections seemed to transport them to a rich aesthetic world of wonder and imagination.

As we continued to discuss our observations of Jessica and Isabella, we recognized that their work exemplified a value that we hold dear: it is imperative to get to know materials well before they can be used to their fullest potential. The girls' deep investigation of the chalk and our curiosity about their process informed the rest of our dialogue. We are grateful to Jessica and Isabella for showing us how much more children see and engage with the sensory world than we imagined. We are now committed to presenting materials with an awareness of their fuller aesthetic possibilities and making time for children to explore them fully as Jessica and Isabella did with the chalk. Whether we observe children using paint, glue, clay, or chalk, we will be eager to see children covering their hands, arms, and faces and then reaching out to each other. From the initial dip of a finger to the colored water running down their arms at clean up, children see that life is meant to be experienced with all of their senses!

Seeing and Appreciating Children's Humor

Babies in the Bath

One morning I offered my toddlers tubs filled with sudsy water so they could give the baby dolls a bath. The children spent quite a bit of time doing what I expected: splashing the water, dunking the babies, and covering them with the sparkly bubbles floating in the tubs. Then, as often happens, one of the children had a new idea. Oona climbed into a tub and looked up with a grin. This idea sparked Caleb to do the same, and the two of them looked at each other sitting in the tubs and began to laugh. Hannah had another plan and she decided to squeeze into the tub with Caleb. Much to Caleb's chagrin, Hannah began to laugh uproariously at what she thought was an even funnier idea.

It was wonderful to see the children engaged in this humorous moment, joining together in enjoyment and laughter. I have often observed children sharing a good laugh, which has sparked my fascination in what children think is humorous and why. As I have been observing for examples of humor, I've also been studying resources about the development of humor in young children. I am curious about the significance of humor in children's development and how my responses to their humor can support their learning and relationships.

Humor is what makes something funny and a sense of humor is the ability to recognize it. Humor is also something that can be learned and in turn, helps make life more enjoyable. Children are developing a sense of humor when they recognize what's funny and can amuse each other as well. I want to support children's innate understanding of the importance of humor for their lives and mine. I have learned that what is funny to toddlers is similar to what makes most of us laugh: noticing and understanding when things are unconventional, unusual, and new. If you think about a comedian that you enjoy, you'll notice that they twist ordinary events in surprising ways that make us laugh.

In studying Jennifer Cunningham's research on the development of humor in children, I see why my toddlers thought getting into the tubs was so funny:

> "A preference for novel events suggests that some of the pleasure of experiencing humorous events stems from children not knowing what to expect. Children's first attempts at humor production reflect this understanding that unexpectedness elicits laughter. Often, the first 'jokes' that a toddler makes are nonverbal attempts to create incongruity, such as placing a toy in her cereal or in her shoe or on her head." [22]

It's no wonder children laugh so often—they have been in the world such a short time and to them almost everything is unexpected, unusual, and unconventional. Adults can learn to laugh with children if we slow down and marvel with them at the wondrous world they see. Humor reflects children's growing understanding of the world around them. Yet, what I notice more is the social nature of humor. Laughing brings more laughing and often the children will laugh with eager anticipation of others joining in. I believe that beyond the learning reflected in humor there is a deep sense of satisfaction that comes from sharing these moments with each other.

"Here We Are"

One morning, a number of my toddlers crowded around the mirror, smiling and laughing as they saw each other's reflections. At one point they seemed to share a moment of total connection, which sparked exuberant laughter and dancing around in a circle. Their laughter was contagious and as they continued to dance and laugh, other children joined in.

Research shows that children laugh approximately 200 times a day, whereas adults laugh only 15-18 times. People who laugh more are healthier, experience less stress, are less likely to be depressed, and may even have an increased resistance to illness or physical problems. The children seem to be on to something that we adults have lost. But why is this so?

For toddlers, laughter seems to come from the pure thrill of shared moments of connection with friends, like laughing and dancing together. My observations of children support the research that shows that laughter is less about humor and more about creating social connections, where people build feelings of camaraderie and pay close attention to each other. Jennifer Cunningham reports:

> "Sharing laughter together often serves as the precursor to other forms of social intimacy. Laughter becomes one of the earliest and most enduring tools for getting to know one another. The humor context is so powerful that it breaks down even difficult social barriers." [23]

Silly Routines!

For preschoolers, humor that helps them connect with each other is often antagonizing to adults. Several years ago, one of my groups of preschoolers used humor to connect with each other and test the boundaries of acceptable behavior. They often chanted and changed the words to some of our songs using "potty talk." Another of their favorite "funny" activities was to clean the snack table by running around and around, faster and faster, wiping with the sponges as they went around. As they moved, they joined together, shouting with gales of laughter. Cunningham explains the children's humor in this situation as follows:

> *"Things that are not OK to say in some situations are somehow safe when we are only joking. The pleasure of humor is in the cognitive realization that the situation is unreal and incongruous with the 'rules' of the world, as we know it. As children begin to use their perceptions and past experiences to formulate expectations about situations and events, they often react with laughter and surprise when these expectations are violated."* [24]

Negotiating Exuberant Connections

Potty talk reflects the type of humor Cunningham describes. It seems the more adults are upset by it, the more hilarious it is for children. They build a sense of camaraderie around "breaking the rules." If we as educators can understand that this humor suggests growth in children's cognitive abilities and social understandings, we may be able to embrace the joy and solidarity it brings to them. If we ignore potty talk, we can take some of the power out of it, perhaps reduce the amount of it children use. Or we can join with them in the pure excitement of their new understandings.

As to the children's silly running game, I can see the power and connection the children felt, but worry about their safety: the children could slip and fall, or bump into furniture and get hurt. What am I communicating when I allow the children to run inside the classroom? While reflecting, I challenge myself to see the children's points of view.

When I pause to really see children, my worries lessen. I come to appreciate the pleasure and friendship these moments bring. I am learning that humor is an important and uniquely human element of communication that helps children build relationships with one another. At the same time, I need to negotiate with the children in this moment to help keep them safe. I can honor the children's innate and skillful desire to connect through humor while guiding them to slow down and watch out for each other as they joyfully clean the table. In the words of Hugh Sidey:

> *"A sense of humor…is needed armor. Joy in one's heart and some laughter on one's lips is a sign that the person down deep has a pretty good grasp of life."*

What Do You Think is Funny and How Often Do You Laugh?

If humor is an antidote for many ills and offers useful benefits, then finding ways to have more of it can brighten our lives. A good sense of humor is a tool that children and adults can rely on throughout life to:

- see things from different perspectives.
- be spontaneous.
- grasp unconventional ways of thinking.
- see beyond the surface of things.
- enjoy and participate in the playful aspects of life.
- not take yourself too seriously.
- build strong relationships and get along with others.[25]

We have a great resource in children when it comes to increasing the humor, laughter, and joy in our lives. Think about the statistic that children laugh 200 times each day. If you are with them even half a day, that is 100 shared laughs a day. All it takes is slowing down to see, and appreciate children's humor!

Seeing Children's Pleasure with Food

> *The art of dining well is no slight art, the pleasure not a slight pleasure.*
>
> ~Michel de Montaigne

Children's relationship with food in early childhood programs is often a complex topic. Families have concerns about "picky eaters" and teachers feel pressure to make sure that children eat enough while in their care. Children bring snacks that teachers describe as junk food and believe this negatively impacts children's behavior. Foods marketed for children are often less than wholesome and childhood obesity is a growing concern among many professionals. Unfortunately, it's also still true that too many children in the United States have limited access to enough healthy food. These issues, as well as regulations governing how often children should eat, what kinds of food, and how much children should be eating, are most often the focus of mealtimes in early childhood programs.

Studying children's perspectives about food can enhance our understandings and inform our actions. When I focus on children's engagement at mealtime rather than pressures and concerns, I find that children bring great pleasure to their experiences with food. If I notice and highlight these positive moments, I more likely will enhance children's healthy relationships with food.

One of my favorite times of day with a group of toddlers is mealtime. The children eagerly gather around the table, anticipating what's to come. It's one of the few times during the day that their usually active bodies are still. This time often has a meditative quality to it as the children sit quietly and immerse themselves fully in the experience. They notice the collection, colors, textures, temperature, and taste of the food. The children explore with their hands and fingers, as well as their mouths.

They eat slowly, picking up single pieces in their fingers, rubbing the food around in their mouths before they chew and swallow. Often they'll chew and chew and chew, savoring every aspect of the crunchy textures or eruption of flavors, and then spit out what's left. I'm always impressed with the children's earnest attempts to master using a spoon. Using one hand, they scoop food with a spoon and at the same time use their other hand and fingers to grasp the pieces of food to get them successfully into their mouths.

I've heard adults discourage this sensory exploration and efficient finger eating when they remind children to "use your spoon" or "stop playing with your food." Instead, I want to delight with and learn from the children's persistence, pleasure, and total captivation with these experiences.

I recently spent time with a close friend and her 17-month-old granddaughter, Elena. Elena's family is bilingual and her word for all food is "agua," which means "water" in Spanish. She exuberantly calls out, "agua, agua, agua" when she sees it's time to eat. Her body quivers with anticipation as she is handed a banana. Her chubby hand grasps and she watches closely as she gently squeezes the fruit. She eagerly puts it into her mouth and rubs the banana around her lips and tongue and then takes a bite. Calm and focus come to her as she eats, and her eyes get a dreamy look of pure satisfaction. When she is offered a handful of mixed grain cereals, she picks up and studies each piece individually before popping it in her mouth, and then purposefully examines the taste and texture as she chews. Next, she takes on the task of scooping yogurt into a spoon and working to get the slippery substance into her mouth. More of the yogurt ends up on her face and bib, but she doesn't seem to care. Instead, she is intent on sucking every bit of cool, creamy taste off the spoon.

My observations of these very young children lead me to believe that they engage in the purest experiences of food for pleasure, as well as sustenance. They haven't yet taken on the negative messages that impact our relationships with food. When we support children to stay tuned-in to their natural appetite, they will know when they are hungry and when they have had enough. If they are offered healthy choices, their unsullied palates find great satisfaction in wholesome, real foods.

Mealtime with preschool children always reminds me of the pleasure of sharing food with others. Children like to discover who likes the same kinds of foods they do. They love to share food with each other as a way to cultivate connections and build friendships. One year, in my preschool class, a number of families were concerned about children sharing the food that was sent from home. We wanted to respect these families' views, so we began reminding the children that their family didn't want them to share their food. The children strongly let us know that this message totally countered our continual reminders to share in every other aspect of preschool. The children rebelled and designated a sharing table, inviting anyone who wanted to share their snack to eat at that table. We told the families about the children's passionate activism and worked together to develop guidelines for sharing food that everyone was happy with.

The children also eagerly share stories of the foods they eat at home. Food is a rich expression of family and culture, so to highlight these conversations helps children come to know themselves and each other better. When the children's families pack their snacks for school, we can have conversations about family rituals and values associated with mealtime. Children are reminded of the bonds they have with their family in the midst of their school day when they open their bag or box and eat the food that mom or dad packed with loving care.

In our busy lives and fast-paced world, slowing down to notice the sweetness of a blueberry bursting in our mouths, the crunchiness of a cracker, the soothing comfort that comes from sipping tomato soup, and the joys, comfort, and bonds that grow when sharing food with others, are gifts we can learn from seeing children's pleasure with food.

Can Babies Read and Write?

Adult concerns about literacy development in early childhood fill the air-waves and have begun to trickle down and impact experiences for children under three. Infomercials promote the notion that "your baby can read," by showing happy babies identifying words on flashcards and toddlers writing letters. My first reaction is dismay for why would someone spend the precious, short time of babyhood forcing attention on isolated literacy skills and drills? But then my curiosity is piqued; the children look joyful and excited to be playing these games. Rather than worrying about what the children are learning, I want to discover what they see and understand about these interactions and the lines and squiggles that we call reading and writing. What is the baby's point of view in these moments?

Recently, I was reviewing a toddler teacher's documentation story describing two-year-old Sofia reading a book to a stuffed animal. As I studied the photos, it was obvious that Sofia knew a lot about reading books. She had carefully placed the animal next to her, purposefully holding the book and turning the pages so the animal could see as she read. I was curious to notice in one of the photos that Sofia was explicitly pointing to the letters in the book. What did someone so young know about letters? When Sofia's mom arrived to pick her up, I described my curiosity and asked her to tell me about Sofia's knowledge of books and letters. She excitedly told me the story of how she and Sofia's older brother do homework each night, focusing on reading, writing, and phonics and Sofia eagerly wants to join in. She told me, "Sofia knows letter sounds now, almost as much as her brother does and she loves to write them too." At that point, she got out her cell phone and proudly showed me multiple photos of Sofia with clipboard and pen, intensely focused on writing lines of letters.

Children Care About What Adults Care About

In my own informal research about children's points of view about reading and writing, what jumps out at me is not the children's interest in pen, paper, and letters, but their palpable joy in connecting with people as they engage in these activities. The adults on television with the babies who can read are smiling, clapping in celebration, and showing total, positive attention to the children during each interaction with the flashcards. It was apparent to me that Sofia's interest and skill in reading and writing came from her desire to be a part of the important "real work" in her family, as well as her mother's pride and attention. Children care about what the significant adults in their lives care about and will do what we think is important.

Make It Meaningful

I've also discovered from my informal research that children pay closer attention to the lines and squiggles of literacy if they are connected to meaningful aspects of their lives. I playfully began to point to and say the letters of my one-year-olds' names on the tags that identified their diaper bin as I was changing diapers. To my surprise and delight the children eagerly took up this game, pointing and repeating the sounds with me.

I would read and point, "H-A-N-N-A-H, Hannah," and then point to her photo next to her name and say, that's your name. Hannah would follow me saying, "hch–hch–hch." Most of the children loved this game, even requesting it by calling out a few sounds when we got to the diaper table. But what did they really understand about the letters? Did they see the connection between themselves and these sounds and squiggles? My best guess was that developmentally, the work the children were doing was learning to speak and make sounds, so this sound game was a perfect match for their interests and ability.

I experimented further by writing the children's names and saying the letters as I wrote when we were exploring markers. Again, the children would imitate me, making lines with the markers as they repeated the letter sounds. Still, I wondered, did they do this because they wanted to further a relationship with me through this fun game, or were they connecting meaning to the marks and sounds and themselves?

After a few months of playing these games, I noticed 22-month-old Oona looking at a book that had the word "LOOK" on the cover. At one point, she glanced at me and pointed to the two "O's" and exclaimed "Oona!" Of course I was all over her with excitement and praise and eagerly told her dad the story when he picked her up. A week later she was painting at the easel, enjoying the movement of her arm and brush, inadvertently making swirling, circle shapes with the paint. She stopped, looked closely, and pointed to the big "O" on her paper and said, "Oona."

I can't say that my focus on letter sounds and writing led to Oona's discoveries, but it has been an engaging process that I will continue studying. I also worry that what I've described here could be perceived as over-emphasizing literacy skills at this young age. That's not my intent. What I've learned from observing my group of one-year-olds is that they are making meaning all of the time. If I make reading and writing a meaningful part of our daily lives, they are just as interested in this as in everything else. I've come to see that what we do together is a part of identity development, not just literacy development. Each child's face can be connected to their name, the sound of it, the letters, and how it is written, as well as to their family name, and their friends' names. Making it meaningful in this way is the most important element.

Adults Have the Power

Adults have all the power in children's lives. We are their window and access to safety, comfort, and engaging experiences. Children are smart enough to know this from the time they are babies. They have laser-like attention to what we care about, and they want to imitate, please, and be a part of what we say and do. If you look at cultures around the world, children learn to do what adults value, and believe children can accomplish because this is what they focus on and take time to teach children to do. But with this power comes responsibility. Young children can learn about literacy if that is what we care about and focus on with eager attention in a playful, loving relationship. But we should ask ourselves: What are we and they missing when we spend so much of our time focused on literacy skills? What about the scientific discoveries and magic in a puddle of water, the complex, creative work of pretend play, the deep, spiritual connections from time together in the natural world, or the adventure and sense of accomplishment in toddling up a hill? Babies can read and write, but should they?

Sharing the Stories of Seeing Children

- The Good-bye Game
- Wherever the Road May Lead: Investigating Pathways
- An Intentional Mess: "The Junkyard"
- "I See You"

Throughout these stories, perhaps you have noticed that looking for the details of children's actions encourages you to question or suspend your judgments and interpretations. This is a critical skill in being able to see children. Children are continually exploring the world to find meaning in the smallest details of the people and the wonders around them. Their brains are open and flexible, which allows them to see and hear more than we do. Adults use past experiences and language to quickly interpret, judge, and make decisions. Our brains are often inflexible. Slowing down to see children offers great pleasure in the moments we share with them. This practice keeps us present in our work, which in turn, helps us stay lively and calm throughout the day. Most teachers who are new to this practice are surprised by what they discover about children's initiative and intention. When you see children's competence and abilities, you are eager to share this with others. You also come to see the powerful role you can play to enhance children's experiences and adult understandings.

Making use of detailed observations comes from pausing and reflecting to decide what meaning they have and the actions you might take up. There are many ways to interpret observations, yet in this climate of assessment and school readiness, we are often limited to focusing on deficits and problems. Once we realize we have the power to collect the details of children's strengths and competencies, we can share stories and take actions that help us live our best selves and highest values. With the pressures we have in our programs and the strife in the world around us, stopping to really see children makes that possible.

The following stories are from teachers who take time to see and share the best of what living and learning with children offers. These stories grew from small details, and reflect lovely moments, deep emotional under-standings, personal insights, changes in practice, and advancing big ideas. My hope is that they will inspire you to find your own stories to grow.

The Good-bye Game

Deb Curtis
Seattle, Washington

> *Notice the details of two-year-old Hannah's game and how Deb was able to see more meaning in it for her own and the child's struggle with the important emotional work of separation.*

I'm curious as I've watched Hannah repeatedly invent a game over the last few weeks. She rounds up purses or baskets, fills them with rocks or loose parts from indoors, and walks to the door if she is inside, or to the gate if outside. From there, she waves, smiles, and cheerfully calls out, "Good-bye, good-bye!" She has been repeating this game again and again.

I'm intrigued by the significance of this good-bye game for Hannah. She struggles with separating from her family each morning and I wonder if the game is her attempt to practice these difficult moments of saying good-bye, while being in charge of them. I think the fact that she is doing the leaving in her game allows her to bring more positive emotions and even a sense of joy to the idea of saying good-bye. She has earnestly replayed this game over and over for several weeks and I think that is why her morning separation is becoming a lot easier.

I marvel at her ability to figure out how to negotiate the big world she is learning to live in. Separation was an issue for me when I was a child and even now I am often anxious when I travel away from home. I'm so glad I have been able to capture these moments of Hannah's day. Her example of making a game out of these scary feelings inspires me. If she can figure these big things out, so can I.

Wherever the Road May Lead: Investigating Pathways

Andrea Parypa
Peterborough, Ontario, Canada

Listen to the following story and study the photos for each detail that Andrea noticed in the children's work. Consider the role she played to make the details visible and how her actions extended the children's investigation, collaboration, and learning.

Two children were quietly placing big wooden blocks together on the carpet to form a path. This play was a common sight in our room that I made note of many times. I had a different plan for this day, but as I saw the children's excitement about the block work, I decided to follow their lead to see what unfolded.

The children began moving their bodies along the block path in various ways and as I watched, I highlighted what I saw—"Eva you're moving along the path with one foot on and one foot off. Look at Ryder's idea. He's pulling himself along the path with his arms!" I noticed that as I announced each movement, the children eagerly began to try them out. Also, the children started to draw attention to their own ideas. Juno shared, "Look! I used the pillow and made a train ride. Choo! Choo!" as she slid along the track on a pillow.

Over several days the children continued to explore different ways to build and travel along the block path. The paths they created were often straight and long until one day, Eva placed the blocks around the pergola post, which changed the course of the play. Several children were challenged by this adjustment to the path and put the blocks back in linear formation. Each time the children moved the blocks back in line, Eva repositioned the blocks around the post. Initially, I remained an observer, wanting to give the children the opportunity to work out this predicament. When they didn't seem to be working it out, I brought the children together to give recognition to both ideas being presented. I said, "Leilana

and Juno, you really like the path to be long and straight. Eva, I noticed you were taking the blocks over to the post. You have a different idea. Let's watch and see what Eva's idea is." With a captive audience, Eva circled the blocks around the post and shared, "So now we can go round and round!" Suddenly, the energy level grew, and the other children excitedly started traveling this new turn in the path. As days passed, I noticed that her peers appreciated Eva's idea as this new element became part of all future path constructions. Likewise, Eva delighted in this recognition, exclaiming proudly—"That be my idea!"

Reflecting on the many ways the children worked with the paths, I noticed that anytime a

block shifted out of line, it was quickly put back in place. Curiosity led me to wonder how the children would respond to a broken path. To provoke the children to think in a fresh way and satisfy my own wonderings, I presented a new challenge to the children. As they began building their path, I joined in and positioned two blocks with a gap between them and exclaimed, "Oh no! Our path has a hole! How will we walk across our path now?" The children were drawn in by my dramatic announcement and eagerly took on this problem. Challenged to think of new possibilities, the children's ingenuity and resourcefulness shone through. Grace confidently stood up and modeled—"I take a biiiggg step." Eva maneuvered herself over the hole by crawling on all fours. As I encouraged the children to look around the room to consider what else we could use to get over the gap, even more ideas were offered. Charlotte filled the hole with pillows and climbed over them. Another time, she filled the gap with foam blocks to walk across. Leilana incorporated a ramp piece to form a bridge to walk across. We took time for the children to share their ideas and for the group to test each one.

As the children revisited this work for many days, the pathway constructions evolved in complexity. New ideas were incorporated into the building designs, which became part of the children's path-building repertoire each day. Throughout this process, I supported the children to share their ideas and negotiate a collaborative vision for the pathways they constructed. The initial linear block path grew to include various materials, follow a winding route that covered the room, and encouraged children to try out new ways to move on the path: over, under, and around many obstacles. By following the initial interest presented by the children, a rich learning journey has been undertaken and continues to evolve. As I reflect on this work, I recognize that although my curiosity may often lead me to present an idea to the children, it is their wonderings and engagement that determine the path we will follow, and it is my response to these observations that will determine the length of our journey.

An Intentional Mess: "The Junkyard"

Nadia Jaboneta
San Francisco, California

> *Nadia's attention to the significance of the details of the children's play has helped change her image of their competence and propelled her to share her new understandings with others. Notice how she talks about the changes she has made in her thinking and practice as a result of seeing children.*

As I walked down the stairs to the yard today, I was delighted to see an amazing creation in progress. At first glance, it looked like a big mess and not too long ago I would have asked the children to stop and clean up. I also might have previously thought that the children were not being respectful of the materials. In fact, what was happening was quite the opposite. Learning to stop and take time to pause and reflect on what is going on has helped me see the children's big ideas come alive.

I stayed nearby and watched as the children created a plan: "I'll collect all the red buckets and you get all the shovels," said Nicolai. Off the

children went, in different directions, pushing the dump trucks at full speed. They carefully determined the placement of the materials before putting each one onto the big pile. They took turns deciding what materials to collect next as the junkyard grew. Other children who showed interest in the pile were happily invited to join the effort.

Since studying schema theory, I now understand that learning is happening when children create "junkyards" and using all the materials in the yard is a necessity. A schema is a thread of thought that is demonstrated by repeated actions

and patterns in children's play. When children are exploring schemas, they are building understandings of abstract ideas, patterns, and concepts.

It is such a wonderful feeling to see the same magic that the children see in the materials. I want to share these feelings with other teachers, so I try to find moments to point out and rave about the competence I am seeing in the children's work. During classroom team meetings, I bring photos of this type of work to closely examine and reflect on. We study the learning, creativity, and theories behind the children's work. We make plans about how we can further support this type of play. We celebrate the brilliance we see in children!

"I See You"

Kate Tucker
Seattle, Washington

> Kate captures this special moment to share with two-year-old Opal and her family through this Welcome Story. Kate's program uses this practice of finding a detailed moment to share to welcome each child into the program. What better message could Kate send to Opal than "I see you."

Dear Opal,

I lay beside you as you woke from your nap. You popped up, pointed to the basket of dolls, and I offered you one. I watched as you enthusiastically cupped your hands around the doll's hair. Next, you carefully studied the doll's shoes and examined the long strands of black strings attached at the top of its head. You repeatedly went back and forth, studying the doll from head to toe, placing it underneath your blanket or laying it on your pillow. You noticed one of the strings had become detached, held it up, looked at me, and smiled. You delicately picked up the string and began to wrap it around your finger in a graceful sweeping motion. You then looked deep into my eyes, pointed to them, and whispered "eyes!" You pointed to the doll's eyes and said, "eyes!" You pointed to your own eyes and said, "eyes!" "I see you Opal," I said.

Opal, while this has only been your second week with us, it feels as though you have been in our classroom from the very start. I thoroughly enjoy watching you vibrate around the classroom with such intention and deep curiosity. We are so excited to have you with us as your infectious energy lights up the room. Your new friends are already asking about you, showing us your family picture, and telling us your name. I so look forward to getting to know you better, along with more post-nap discoveries.

Warmly yours,
Kate

CONCLUSION
Find Your Inspiration

Through this collection of stories, I hope you understand the power of slowing down to notice the children you spend your days with. When you do this, I can guarantee you will find more meaning and enjoyment in your work. And what better message to give children than Kate's words in the last story: "I see you."

I am grateful to the children who have spent their days with me sharing their remarkable view of the world, as well as to my son Casey, who helped me see more than I ever imagined. I also want to thank the remarkable teachers who were willing to share their stories. I am indebted to others who have inspired me to slow down and see children, including the educators from the schools of Reggio Emilia, Italy, who have brought us the important concept of the power of our "image of the child"; Dr. Elizabeth Jones and Dr. Elizabeth Prescott, my professors at Pacific Oaks College, who many years ago inspired my journey to collect the "ordinary gems" of children's play and see the rich meaning in them; and special thanks to my friend and work partner Margie Carter, who continues to eagerly listen to the hours of stories I have told her about children. I hope you find your inspiration to keep seeing children at the center of your work.

Endnotes

1 Joe Lasker, *Mothers Can Do Anything* (Chicago: A. Whitman, 1979).

2 Deb Curtis and Margie Carter, *Learning Together with Young Children: A Curriculum Framework for Reflective Teachers,* 2nd ed. (St. Paul, MN: Redleaf Press, 2017).

3 Barbara Lehn, *What is a Scientist?* (Brookfield, CT: Millbrook Press, 1999).

4 Alison Gopnik, *The Philosophical Baby: What Children's Minds Tell Us About Truth, Love, and the Meaning of Life* (New York: Picador, 2010).

5 Nikolien van Wijk and Gillian Christie, *Getting Started With Schemas: Revealing the Wonder-full World of Children's Play* (Waitakere, NZ: New Zealand Playcentre Federation, 2008).

6 Alison Gopnik, Andrew N. Meltzoff, and Patricia K. Kuhl, *The Scientist In the Crib: What Early Learning Tells Us About the Mind* (New York: HarperPerennial, 2001); Gopnik, *Philosophical Baby.*

7 William M. Schafer, "The Infant as Reflection of Soul: The Time Before There Was a Self." *Zero to Three (J)* 24:3 (2004): 4-8.

8 Mara Davoli, Gino Ferri, and Carla Rinaldi, *Reggio Tutta: A Guide to the City by the Children.* (Reggio Emilia, Italy: Reggio Children, 2014).

9 Schafer, 4-8.

10 Gopnik, *Philosophical Baby.*

11 Marilou Hyson, *Enthusiastic and Engaged Learners: Approaches to Learning In the Early Childhood Classroom* (New York: Teachers College Press, 2008).

12 Nancy Shute, *For Kids, Self-Control Factors Into Future Success,* www.npr.org/2011/02/14/133629477/for-kids-self-control-factors-into-future-success (2011).

13 Ellen Galinsky, *Mind In the Making: The Seven Essential Life Skills Every Child Needs* (New York: HarperStudio, 2010).

14 Gopnik, *Philosophical Baby.*

15 Carol Garhart Mooney, *Theories of Childhood: an introduction to Dewey, Montessori, Erikson, Piaget, and Vygotsky,* 2nd ed. (St. Paul, MN: Redleaf Press, 2013).

[16] Deb Curtis, and Margie Carter, *Designs for Living and Learning: Transforming Early Childhood Environments,* 2nd ed. (St. Paul, MN: Redleaf Press, 2015).

[17] Karen Katz, *I Can Share!* (New York: Grosset & Dunlap, 2011).

[18] Tom Drummond, *Enterprise Talk: A Handrail to Integrity and Authenticity,* http://tomdrummond.com/leading-and-caring-for-children/enterprise-talk/ (2017).

[19] Mihaly Csikszentmihalyi, *Flow: The Psychology of Optimal Experience* (New York: HarperPerennial, 2009).

[20] Gopnik, *Philosophical Baby.*

[21] van Wijk and Christie, *Getting Started With Schemas.*

[22] Cunningham, J. "Children's Humor" *Children's Play.* 93. (Thousand Oaks, CA: Sage Publications, 2004).

[23] Ibid., p. 95.

[24] Ibid., p. 97.

[25] Kids Health from Nemours, *Encouraging Your Child's Sense of Humor,* http://kidshealth.org/parent/growth/learning/child_humor.html (2015).

Deb Curtis is a passionate advocate for childhood and children, and the adults who care for and educate them. She has spent over 40 years working with children and teachers in early childhood programs throughout North America, Australia, and New Zealand. She is the co-author of several books related to working with children and adults in early childhood settings. Deb currently works as a teacher at Epiphany Early Learning Preschool in Seattle, Washington.